Drug Smugglers on Drug Smuggling

Drug Smugglers
on
Drug Smuggling

Lessons from the Inside

Scott H. Decker and
Margaret Townsend Chapman

TEMPLE UNIVERSITY PRESS
Philadelphia

TEMPLE UNIVERSITY PRESS
1601 North Broad Street
Philadelphia PA 19122
www.temple.edu/tempress

⊛ The paper used in this publication meets the requirements of the American
National Standard for Information Sciences—Permanence of Paper for Printed
Library Materials, ANSI Z39.48–1992

Library of Congress Cataloging-in-Publication Data

Decker, Scott H.
    Drug smugglers on drug smuggling : lessons from the inside / Scott H.
Decker and Margaret Townsend Chapman.
        p. cm.
    Includes bibliographical references and index.
    ISBN 13: 978-1-59213-642-1   ISBN 10: 1-59213-642-7 (cloth: alk paper)
    ISBN 13: 978-1-59213-643-8   ISBN 10: 1-59213-643-5 (pbk.: alk paper)
    1. Drug traffic. 2. Drug dealers. I. Chapman, Margaret Townsend, 1972–
II. Title.
    HV5801.D415 2008
    363.45–dc22   2007022654

2 4 6 8 9 7 5 3 1

Contents

    in the Drug Smuggling Trade ▪ 88
        Drug Smuggling Roles ▪ 89
        Recruitment into Drug Smuggling ▪ 95
        Motivation for Drug Smuggling ▪ 104
        Leaving Drug Smuggling ▪ 109
        Summary ▪ 111

6   Balancing Risk and Reward ▪ 114
        Minimizing Risks ▪ 114
        Avoiding Detection ▪ 117
        Changes in Smuggling Activities in Response to Risk ▪ 123
        Getting Caught ▪ 127
        Assessing Risk ▪ 133
        Perceptions of the U.S. Criminal Justice System ▪ 136
        If You Were in Charge ▪ 141
        Summary ▪ 143

7   Making Sense of Drug Smuggling:
    Conclusions and Summary ▪ 145
        Organizational Structure ▪ 146
        Managing Risk ▪ 151
        Potential Responses by Law Enforcement ▪ 154

    Appendix 1. Instrumentation Study Design ▪ 163

    Appendix 2. Study Design ▪ 181

    Notes ▪ 199

    References ▪ 203

    Index ▪ 207

Acknowledgments

We are grateful to the Office of National Drug Control Policy (ONDCP), U.S. Coast Guard (USCG), and U.S. Customs Service, who funded the research presented in this book. In particular, Commander John Manning, U.S. Navy, Dr. Michael Cala from ONDCP, Senior Special Agent Fred Stacey of the U.S. Customs Service, and Commander Brian Kelley, USCG, were all instrumental to the success of our work. We also extend special thanks to staff at the U.S. Sentencing Commission and the Bureau of Prisons, without whose cooperation the interviews would not have been accomplished. Lastly, we would like to thank our colleagues at Abt Associates, who provided invaluable support. We would like to express special thanks to Mary Layne, William Rhodes, Caben Chester, Gary Schaffer, and John Lavin.

Drug Smugglers on Drug Smuggling

1 Motivation for the Study

D rug use is a major issue in the United States. Prior research has linked it to a host of social ills, including involvement in crime, destabilization and decline of neighborhoods, and family instability. In addition, drug importation represents a major threat to the political security of both the United States and source countries and impedes economic development in countries where drugs are grown in large quantities. Although studies of drug use are numerous and our understanding of local drug markets is growing, our understanding of the multimillion-dollar business of international drug smuggling is considerably less well developed.

This book examines drug smuggling from the perspective of those most in the know—experienced drug smugglers. Ironically, most of what we know about drug smuggling comes from minor players who are involved in the international drug trade. Information from interviews with individuals heavily involved in the drug trade should provide important information for crafting interdiction strategies. A major focus of this book is to understand the steps drug smugglers take in reducing their risks of being caught, losing a load, or being ripped off. In this regard, behavioral change on the part of smugglers can take one of two major paths: They may be deterred by increased risks of being caught, or they may alter their behavior in ways that increase their costs of doing business and make the smuggling of drugs either less profitable or more susceptible to interdiction.

A better understanding of how individuals respond to increased risk is of considerable importance owing to the significance of drug use in the United States as well as the annual expenditure on drug enforcement and treatment. More than fifty agencies in the federal government are involved in drug supply-and-demand reduction strategies, and the annual budget of these agencies is approximately $17 billion. It is estimated that when federal, state, and local expenditures are combined, the United States spends roughly $30 billion annually on drug control efforts (Abt Associates, 1999: 4). In addition, drug smuggling has been linked in some circles to terrorism.

There are two specific goals that focus on interdiction efforts in the National Drug Control Strategy (NDCS). The first is to shield America's air, land, and sea frontiers from the drug threat. This includes a target of reducing the rate at which illegal drugs cross the transit and arrival zones by 20 percent. Strategies include the detection, disruption, deterrence, and seizure of illegal drugs in transit; the development of technology to aid in this strategy; and the improvement of relations with Caribbean and Central American nations. The second goal for reducing the supply of drugs is to achieve a 30 percent reduction in the amount of drugs shipped from producer nations and a 50 percent reduction in illicit drugs produced in the United States. Strategies to support this goal include disrupting and dismantling major smuggling organizations; arresting, prosecuting, and incarcerating leaders; supporting drug enforcement and political structures in source countries; reducing money laundering; and encouraging research. Such efforts should introduce considerable levels of risk into the drug smuggler's calculus of the cost of doing business.

To date, most knowledge of drug smuggling has come from a limited number of sources. Many of the sources are government agencies involved in the effort to increase interdiction and stem the flow of narcotics importation into the United States. At best, these data provide a limited picture of the volume of drugs smuggled each year, the methods engaged in by drug smugglers, and the perceived impact of changes in interdiction strategy on the behavior of smugglers.

This book seeks to fill that void through in-depth interviews with the most heavily involved drug smugglers incarcerated in the federal prison system. The authors were afforded access to thirty-four of the highest-level drug smugglers confined in federal institutions at the time of the study. Intensive interviews provided information on the smugglers' experiences transporting drugs into the United States, their perception of U.S. interdiction activities, their reaction to these activities, and their perception of the risks associated with smuggling drugs into the United States. The authors were fortunate to have received support from the Office of National Drug Control Policy, the U.S. Customs Service, and the U.S. Coast Guard to conduct this work.[1] The cooperation of these and other federal agencies (the U.S. Sentencing Commission and the Bureau of Prisons) is testament to the value placed on what we can learn from the smugglers.

The information gained through this work is particularly important given the magnitude of the problem of drug production. The volume of cocaine production in the source countries of Peru, Bolivia, and Colombia was estimated at roughly 680 metric tons in 1997 (Abt Associates, 1999: 14; United Nations, 2005). Estimates developed by Abt Associates indicate that approximately 300 metric tons of cocaine entered the United States in 1997, roughly 44 percent of the total production tonnage. While there is concern about the use of these figures as precise estimates (Rhodes, Layne, Johnston, and Hozik, 2000), they provide rough gauges against which the magnitude of cocaine importation can be understood.

Understanding Drug Smuggling

Our work is premised on the belief that key knowledge about drug smuggling comes from those who smuggle drugs. To date, most of our understanding of drug smuggling and the impact of drug interdiction policy on smugglers comes from the perspective of those charged with the task of intercepting, arresting, and prosecuting smugglers and low-level dealers. There have been notably few studies of drug smuggling and the impact of interdiction efforts from the perspective of the people involved in the process—the drug smugglers most heavily involved.

Reuter and Haaga (1989) conducted the first notable study involving interviews with drug smugglers in 1987. They asked a total of ninety-four randomly selected inmates at five federal correctional facilities to participate.[2] Forty-one (42 percent) of those who were approached agreed to be interviewed, with higher than average refusal rates among black and Hispanic inmates. Despite the fact that forty-one inmates agreed to be interviewed, only thirty-two of the interviewed subjects were actual drug dealers; three of them were heroin dealers; twenty were cocaine dealers; and nine were marijuana dealers. Of the cocaine dealers, only two made purchases of more than ten kilograms, and four of the twenty were identified as importers who brought cocaine into the United States. Of the marijuana dealers, five were identified as importers, two of whom had purchased more than a ton of marijuana at their last arrest.

Interviews were conducted with English-speaking inmates exclusively, as no translator was available. In addition, interviewers took notes during the interviews rather than recording and transcribing the results. Reuter and Haaga described a variety of reasons for interview refusals, including reluctance to discuss the past, ongoing legal challenges to their incarceration, concerns over the confidentiality of the interviews, and anger at the government's treatment of them in the past. Despite these concerns, Reuter and Haaga concluded: "With a few exceptions, the information from the interviews was plausible, internally consistent, and consistent with the PSR (presentence report) information"

(728). They concluded that their study provided data with suitable internal and external validity.

The Reuter and Haaga study examined four substantive areas of interest. The first was entry into and progression up the ranks of drug smuggling. The authors were particularly interested in learning about the ease—or difficulty—of penetrating drug markets and moving up in the ranks of smuggling organizations. The second research question focused on the nature of the organization behind high-level drug dealing. Here organizational structure and process questions were assessed. The third research issue examined the need to use violence to successfully engage in drug dealing at high levels. Finally, Reuter and Haaga examined the extent to which wholesale drug markets are regional, rather than national, markets.

The drug markets these subjects described were characterized by entry and succession that was less formal, less structured, and with fewer barriers than might be suspected. Individuals were able to enter high-level drug smuggling with few roadblocks and move up the ranks with relative ease. This was true for individuals who assumed positions of trust in organizations and were responsible for handling large sums of money, drugs, or both. The pathways to involvement in smuggling generally led from low-level dealing or handling small loads to large deals. Most subjects reported that the willingness to tolerate risk was a key to being successful, and while many were involved in other forms of crime, roughly the same number worked at legitimate employment. Spanish-language ability and having family members in the business also enhanced introduction and escalation in the sales of drugs at these higher levels. In sum, there appeared to be little in the way of technical requirements, specific skills, and apprenticeships prior to ascending to higher levels of drug sales.

The second issue was the extent to which high-level drug smuggling involved an organizational structure. Reuter and Haaga reported that many subjects used the word *organization* to describe their operations, but they found little evidence that the groups of individuals involved in drug smuggling represented formal organizations that could be compared to corporations or organized crime. Some evidence was found for hierarchical organizations, but this was not universal, and hierarchical organizations did not seem necessary to achieving success or profit at high levels of drug dealing. Few special skills were found among the dealers interviewed for the study, and there was little evidence of information sharing or coordination of efforts across the loosely federated individuals involved in drug markets. Reuter and Haaga concluded that little in the way of importing or distributing drugs, even at the highest levels, required a well-coordinated organization. Rather, high-level drug importation and distribution was a series of transactions between otherwise unconnected independent groups with little structure or permanence. These groups were described as "chains" that link one task in importation or distribution, without corresponding links with parts of the chain involved in other aspects of importation or distribution. Most chains appear to have been small and were formed to accomplish specific tasks, preventing the formation of formal organizations of an enduring or effective nature.

There was little evidence that violence was necessary for success. Indeed, Reuter and Haaga argue that violence is not a key feature of dealing at the high levels of drug markets, unlike much street-level drug dealing. Few of the subjects reported being threatened by violence, though it is worth noting that most of the subjects were recruited from low-security penal institutions, and involvement in violence could disqualify an individual from being sent to such penal institutions.

The final area the authors explored was the geographic boundaries of the illegal drug market. They concluded that the market was national, rather than regional, in scope. This was based on prisoners' reports about the lack of barriers to selling in geographic markets other than those in which they traditionally operated and the experiences of a small number of dealers who managed to deal drugs at a high level in different regions of the country.

Reuter and Haaga drew several conclusions that were important in formulating our work. First, they noted that while the subject refusal rate was a continuing concern, future interviews in higher-level security prisons and presumably with higher-level drug smugglers were likely to yield valuable information.[3] They also argued that the use of prison populations was important to understanding high-level drug markets. Second, they found that even at the top of these markets there was little evidence of formal organization. This finding was viewed as problematic for enforcement efforts, since increasing the risk of arrest and imprisonment was made more difficult by the relative lack of organization. Reuter and Haaga concluded that enforcement efforts that increase the "price" of high-level drug selling are likely to yield benefits. From our perspective, this conclusion is based on too few importers, too many low-level drug dealers, and lack of Spanish-speaking inmates. As a consequence, it is best viewed as a first but important step in learning about international drug smuggling.

Rockwell International (1989) conducted the second major study of high-level drug selling and smuggling based on responses of inmates. Two hundred fifty-four inmates from ten prisons (nine federal institutions and one state prison) were approached to participate in a study of drug smuggling deterrence; one hundred twelve consented to participate. The Federal Bureau of Prisons granted access to institutions with security levels of 1 through 4, though only 20 percent of the Rockwell sample was located in prisons at levels 3 and 4.[4] All inmates who agreed to participate were obliged to sign consent forms.[5]

Just over half the inmates were U.S. citizens; 14 percent were from Mexico; 17 percent were from Colombia; and 14 percent were from other nations. Subjects in their forties accounted for two-fifths of the total. As a group, the smugglers in this study had relatively few years of smuggling experience: 69 percent had smuggled for less than five years prior to their arrest.

The goal of this study was to determine deterrents (i.e., risks) to drug smuggling activities. For the purposes of the study, "deterrence is defined as that level of risk created when interdiction efforts are successful" (Rockwell International, 1989: 3). The premise behind this approach to deterrence is that when risks of detection and apprehension for transportation and importation are increased, the costs of smuggling will be increased. The study also was premised on the belief that increasing smugglers' perceptions of the probability of apprehension and imprisonment is a key to deterrence. Increasing such perceived risks, it is theorized, will lead to increased costs and ultimately to a reduction in drug smuggling efforts.

To measure these perceptions, interview data were collected about the individual inmates' perceptions of risks to themselves and to their associates (individuals known to the inmates). Questions were posed about the potential impact on smuggling under varying levels of certainty of interdiction, imprisonment, gain, and risk. Initially, the study concluded that the concept of deterrence itself could be measured in valid ways.

Inmates in this sample reported that they believe the average risk of successful apprehension to be 30 percent, though they reported that an associate's risk of interdiction was 13.5 percent. The "tipping point"—the point at which the decision would be made to not smuggle drugs—occurred when the risk of apprehension was at 40 percent. However, caution should be used in interpreting these data, as only four data points were allowed in the questionnaire. Thus, an artificial set of decision criteria were offered to subjects, and their responses were fit into a truncated set of response alternatives that may not represent the variety or range of decisions they made. In every case, inmates indicated that their associates were more likely to smuggle at a given level of risk or reward than they were themselves. The authors concluded that the responses for associates were likely the more reliable, as individual offenders would underestimate their own probabilities and offer more realistic responses for the associates. Many of the response scenarios required subjects to calculate two sets of percentages (risk versus reward) for themselves and associates. This required both using a complicated set of decision-making criteria and thinking in strict quantitative terms. Previous work with offenders (Wright and Decker, 1994; 1997) has documented the difficulty most offenders have thinking in quantitative terms. For example, the Rockwell study takes offenders through a four-sequence response scenario in which they are asked to determine whether they would smuggle drugs for a four-level reward scale versus a four-level risk scale. Functionally, this requires offenders to determine sixteen different risk and reward combinations, a difficult proposition.

The Rockwell study also offered several qualitative findings. First, drug smugglers who moved larger quantities of drugs reported that they could reduce the risk of apprehension through planning and care. Second, high-level smugglers told interviewers that the interdiction efforts of the U.S. government were generally well publicized and did not require much sophistication to detect. The interviews also provided a view of a typical smuggling operation. Operations consisted of one or two people who were responsible for setting up the deal, two to four people in transportation, and between four and six individuals who would offload the drugs. As the report notes, "Inmates were all to [*sic*] quick to put down the 'Organized Crime' theory of large criminal families and stated almost all smuggler organizations contained 10 people or less" (Rockwell International, 1989: 30). This theme is important to our own work.

The Institute for Defense Analysis (IDA, 1999) conducted a study examining "the effectiveness of the Frontier Shield pulse operation to deter drug trafficking in and around Puerto Rico," assessing the balance between threshold interdiction rates and drug smuggling deterrence. This study used the Rockwell methodology of estimating deterrence as a gauge of the success of interdiction efforts. The author noted that cocaine is very cheap to grow and that most of the costs associated with cocaine trafficking are importation costs. This study hypothesized that "drug traffickers operate at the lowest cost for the perceived risk" (73). The authors argued that seizures alone are not the best measure of deterrence; rather, the behavior of traffickers themselves is the key to understanding deterrent effects.

The IDA study identified four levels of apprehension rates: (1) lethal apprehension rate, (2) personal apprehension rate, (3) apprehension rate of associates, and (4) vehicle and drug loss rate with no apprehension. The study also differentiated among deterrence in a source zone, in a transit zone, and in a production zone. The IDA study concluded that initial interdiction efforts in major source zones or production sectors produce the greatest deterrent effects. In addition, the study found that deterring air transport of drugs was between ten and a hundred times more effective in disrupting supply levels than previous studies had established.[6]

The study concluded that when 2 percent of drugs that were shipped were interdicted, a threshold for deterring drug interdiction was reached. Any risk at or below that level was perceived to be part of the cost of doing business. When risks exceeded that level, authorities began to get the attention of smugglers. In contrast, arrest of associates, loss of personal property, or loss of drugs required much higher thresholds of apprehension to produce deterrent effects. The study concluded that merely seizing more drugs in the absence of arrests was unlikely to produce deterrent results, since smugglers regarded such losses as part of the cost of doing business. However, to the extent that interdiction was focused on arrest, it was likely to produce deterrent effects.

Griffith (1997) examined the role of drugs in the Caribbean more broadly and also examined the relationship of drug trafficking to political sovereignty in that region. He contended that drug smuggling and the economies that such activities create provide serious threats to the sovereignty of Caribbean nations. Griffith addressed three key questions: (1) the nature and extent of drug dealing in the Caribbean, (2) efforts to combat the problem, and (3) the implications of drug smuggling for security and sovereignty. Griffith argued that the intersection of drug smuggling and national security provides a unique opportunity to examine the role of drug smuggling. He viewed the interaction of drugs, geography, power, and politics as key to understanding the security of the region, and he defined security in a broader context, including military, political, economic, and environmental security in his consideration of the role of drugs in the Caribbean.

This is particularly important in this region because, as he argued, "drug corruption subverts political security" (710). In addition, for many of these nations, the value of drug trafficking transactions exceeds the combined value of all other exports. Such an economic imbalance creates political instability and undermines the ability of elected officials to govern.

The Caribbean is an especially important area for understanding drug smuggling because of its proximity to source and destination countries as well as its long history as a site for smuggling illegal goods and for piracy. Griffith noted that the physical and social geography of the region makes it especially conducive to drug trafficking. This region is the vortex between North and South America and sits between the major source of supply and the major source of demand for drugs. Countless islands, cays, and shielded coasts make for easy access for smugglers and provide excellent cover for storing goods, fitting ships, and offloading transshipments of drugs. The recent sovereignty of many nations in the Caribbean region makes them less capable of responding to the transshipment of drugs because of ill-developed legal systems, inadequate resources and assets, the presence of large-scale corruption, inadequate financial resources, or a combination of those factors. In addition, the economies of many of these nations do not adequately support the populace, making participation in the illegal economy attractive.

Griffith provided extensive descriptions of the nature of drug smuggling operations in the Caribbean. He interviewed government officials, individuals charged with responding to shipments of illegal drugs, and some smugglers. He described the organization of such shipping as a paradox; that is, such groups have sophisticated planning, technology, and communications, yet they themselves are not well organized vertically, and they appear to exhibit few characteristics of formal organizations such as permanence, a command structure, effective communication between ranks, and resource management.

Griffith characterized traffickers as adaptive individuals who pay close attention to countermeasures taken by governments to interdict drug shipments. Citing U.S. State Department reports from 1991 through 1995, he documented a decline in the volume (in kilos) of cocaine shipments of nine Caribbean countries, but he noted that these declines may have reflected the shift in transport strategies of smugglers rather than successful deterrence. Griffith estimated that the interdiction capture rate is between 15 and 25 percent of all shipments for the Caribbean.

The work of Damian Zaitch (2002) is an ambitious attempt to understand cocaine smuggling from Colombia. Zaitch's specific interest was in the smuggling of cocaine from Colombia to the Netherlands, especially the involvement of Surinamese and Dutch natives. A total of forty-four individuals involved in cocaine trafficking were interviewed between 1996 and 1999. Fieldwork was conducted in Amsterdam, the Hague, and Rotterdam in the Netherlands and Bogotá and Cali in Colombia. Zaitch identified five different roles: couriers, importers, distributors, retailers, and helpers. His findings are particularly instructive as they represent a field sample of drug smugglers. His study is couched in the theoretical tradition of studies of organized crime.

This research was ostensibly a study of organized crime, and Zaitch concluded that cocaine smuggling lacks many of the features typically associated with organized crime. Indeed, he argued that most smuggling involves small groups that are isolated from each other, that smuggling lacks vertical organization, and that "families" (individuals with familial ties or long histories of working with each other) are the primary social organizations involved in drug smuggling. Zaitch argued that "cocaine enterprises in themselves are heterogeneous and the mutating product of fragile agreements between people and flexible articulation between legal and illegal enterprises" (7285). Indeed, he described drug smuggling from Colombia to the Netherlands (Europe's second most popular country of destination) as informal, small, and decentralized. The role of family is particularly important in this context. In the end, Zaitch described drug smuggling organizations as not well organized and not resembling the model of organized crime assumed to be the case by most Americans.

According to Zaitch, drug smuggling is a very opportunistic and flexible enterprise.

Astorga (2001) used historical data to describe drug trafficking in Mexico, also exploring similarities between smuggling and organized crime operations. His work characterized drug trafficking as a dynamic enterprise that is flexible in adapting to changes in political and economic forces as well as to interdiction efforts. He characterized efforts to describe drug trafficking as highly organized or as similar to organized crime as "myths" (71) and underscored the transitions in smuggling and smugglers' methods in response to both interdiction efforts and sociopolitical forces.

Impact of Drug Interdiction Efforts

A limited number of studies have examined the impact of interdiction and eradication efforts on drug smuggling. This is, of course, a difficult enterprise, as it requires measuring changes in drug production, drug prices, and transit routes and costs.

Reuter, Crawford, and Cave (1988) measured the impact of increased military participation in interdiction efforts and concluded that increasing the resources available to the military for this purpose is not likely to reduce significantly the availability of cocaine. They argued that only 10 percent of the cost of cocaine comes from transportation and, consequently, that increasing these costs is unlikely to drive smugglers out of the business or substantially increase their costs of doing business. The work of Rydell and Everingham (1994) confirmed that interdiction efforts had little or no effect on reducing the level of smuggling or the cost of cocaine. Even herbicide spraying was found to have little success in reducing the availability of cocaine (General Accounting Office, 1999). Two years of far-ranging herbicide spraying of cocaine in Colombia did not result in declines in coca production; indeed, production increased 50 percent at the conclusion of the two-year period.

Because these studies measured deterrence in terms of drug production and seizures, there is concern that the impact of interdiction may be underestimated. In an effort to address this concern, Caulkins, Crawford, and Reuter (1993) modeled a smuggler response to interdiction efforts. They concluded that in order to achieve any deterrent effect, all routes available to smugglers must be heavily disrupted. A similar study undertaken by Evidence Based Research (1995) found that increases in interdiction resources produced very small reductions in the success of interdiction efforts as measured in the number of seizures.

A related approach examined the effect of interdiction efforts on drug prices. The premise underlying such an approach is that measuring the direct response of drug producers and transporters is difficult because such data are fraught with measurement error. An alternative approach is to measure changes in the cost of drugs. This approach argues that successful interdiction efforts increase the cost of drugs by making transporters take alternative steps, change routes, employ more lookouts, use more sophisticated technology, and tolerate more seized loads. As a consequence of increased interdiction efforts, the costs of doing business and consequently the costs of drugs will escalate. Johnston, Rhodes, Carrigan, and Moe (1999) determined that price sensitivity to interdiction efforts varied by transit zone and other factors, but that overall it was difficult to conclude that interdiction was directly related to price increases. However, Layne, Rhodes, and Chester (2000) found support for the link between interdiction efforts and the price of the drug on the street. Using data provided by the U.S. Customs Service, they estimated the increase in the cost of transporting cocaine attributable to interdiction efforts. Based on reports of investigations from Customs, the study examined the impact of enforcement personnel, aircraft, and technologies on the price of cocaine. The authors found a direct relationship between enforcement activities and the costs of transportation. Specifically, each dollar spent on Customs enforcement produced a corresponding increase of thirty-seven cents in the cost of transportation.

Riley (1993) summarized one response to this line of research by expressing skepticism that interdiction efforts achieve their goal. He argued that the combination of low production costs, high mobility within the cocaine industry, and the ability to respond quickly to changes in enforcement policy combine to frustrate the best efforts at interdiction.

Summary

These studies taken together provide some insights into drug smuggling organizations, methods used to transport drugs, and deterrence capabilities for drug interdiction efforts. This brief review has established several common themes, including smuggler organizational structure, smuggler intelligence, and deterrence.

First, a number of the studies (Reuter and Haaga, Rockwell, IDA, Griffith, and Zaitch) noted the lack of organizational structure that characterizes drug smuggling organizations. The observation that even high-level international drug smuggling lacks many of the characteristics of formal organizational structure is common to much research on the organization of criminal enterprises (e.g., Best and Luckenbill, 1994; Decker, Bynum, and Weisel, 1998). Ianni's (1974) description of organized crime indicated that the organizational ties between individuals in group enterprises are of short duration, involve transactions of an immediate or time-bound nature, lack permanence, and fail to create lasting commitments to a larger organization. This description is similar to what the research has found regarding drug organizations.

Key to understanding the nature of social organizations is following the flow of information (Burt, 1992; Arquilla and Ronfeldt, 1997). In networks of individuals who are loosely connected to each other, interact on a one-time basis, and know of each other through third parties, there is little permanence to the flow of information and less ability to subject information to quality control. We characterize such groups of individuals as informally based, temporally bounded, and loosely coupled. Williams argued that much of the inability of interdiction efforts to achieve better results stems from "the failure to understand fully the structure of these networks and their capacity to counter or circumvent law enforcement and military interdiction" (1998: 154).

The view that dominates current conceptualization of drug smuggling organizations describes vertically integrated structures that resemble the dominant corporate structures following World War II. However, as Burt (1992) and Williams (1998) observed, there are many cells within formal organizations—from drug smuggling, to money laundering, to terrorist groups—that have access to information and technology that allow them to operate independently, often in ways that the organizational heads do not know about, do not understand, and certainly cannot control. Williams argued that the key to understanding such groups is to view them as networks, as a series of loosely connected nodes (individuals, organizations, firms, and information-sharing tools) that are linked across and within organizations. These links are often of short duration and primarily task-specific. From this view, it is impossible to trace a straight vertical line from the bottom of an organization that houses the largest number of workers to decision makers at the top. Indeed, groups that are organized in this fashion may be incapable of developing a more formal structure, as they lack the necessary characteristics to do so.

Networks can be linked within and across organizations and between and within functions, and they can even include competitors. Many networks are self-contained units with no physical contact involving individuals in other parts of the network. The insularity of these nodes is a useful conceptual framework for understanding the drug smuggling process. Networks can cut across a variety of political, linguistic, legal, and geographic barriers in ways that formal organizations cannot. Because of their insular and self-contained nature, networks can be more difficult to penetrate and deter than are large organizations. In a large organization, it may be possible to "flip" one individual and move up—or down—the chain of command. In a series of interconnected networks, it may be impossible to move from one network to another because individuals may not know each other, may not have information about the identity of individuals in other networks, or may just represent the end of a network. Such networks are dynamic and capable of rapid change because they are based not on an existing structure but on the transfer of information (Abt Associates, 1999). For example, when one source for the transportation of drugs is eliminated, it is an easy matter to contract with another source outside the network of the first transporter.

Williams (1998) noted the comparative advantage of such networks over more formal organizations. In a sense, such networks are not trapped by their structure and history and can adapt to environmental changes more quickly. In part, some of the virtue of this form of organization reflects the ideal characteristics provided by "loosely coupled" organizations (Perrow, 1999), in which networks often come together to accomplish a single purpose and may disband or reconnect in the future. Such networks can respond to losses or threats more quickly and efficiently than can organizations that are more tightly coupled and must "re-grow" connections or functions that may be impaired by arrest, conviction, or seizure of assets or by changes in the nature or level of interdiction. Evidence of this can be seen in the rapid transition from the dominance of the Medellin cartel, to the Cali cartels, and to the current offices that independently operate the drug trade in Colombia (DEA, 1997). In such networks, it is likely that individuals involved in a particular function do not know individuals in another function, making penetrating the networks and gathering intelligence about them all the more complicated. A report by Observatoire Geopolitique (1998) confirmed the trend toward further decentralization of larger networks of drug smuggling organizations into smaller units and the increasing presence of "short networks," small, self-contained groups linked only by function and need. It is not simply that organizations are getting smaller and more insular but that they are linked only by function, information, and immediate need with little permanent structure and durability of functional integration. This shift in smuggler organizations to small networks certainly changes traditional enforcement strategies that rely on infiltrating organizations at the lower level in an effort to investigate and eventually arrest major players.

Second, there is evidence that the dynamic nature of drug smuggling networks and the ease with which smugglers learn of

U.S. interdiction activities enable smugglers to avoid detection by changing their routes, methods, or tactics. There is ample evidence that both sophisticated and unsophisticated surveillance strategies—ranging from expensive global positioning systems on the one extreme to simple lookouts on the other—are employed by smugglers. Clearly, the presence of such counterintelligence on the part of drug smugglers represents one of the largest challenges to interdiction efforts.

Finally, the literature supports the notion some drug smuggling is deterred, but there is less agreement on how to measure the amount. One of the dilemmas in deterrence research is that it poses the question, "What would have happened if some event was not present?" Measuring what would have happened in the absence of intervention is difficult. It is useful to think of the deterrence that results from an intervention as operating on a continuum. At one end of the continuum, it is useful to imagine the level of smuggling in the absence of any interdiction effort. Here, drug smugglers would be free to move their supplies as they pleased, limited only by climate, market, and competition. The other end of the continuum would be perfect deterrence, where the level and sophistication of interdiction efforts would successfully deter all efforts to transport drugs. Such a system would have to combine certainty of detection and arrest with certainty of conviction and appropriately severe penalties. Implicit in such a calculus is the notion that the costs would exceed the benefits of smuggling (e.g., cash, thrills, relationships) by enough to prevent anyone from taking part in smuggling.

Of course, we know that perfect deterrence does not exist but that interdiction efforts do produce some level of deterrence. The presence of strong demand for drugs in the United States creates powerful incentives for smuggling. The margin of profit adds to the attractiveness of drug smuggling as well, as perhaps does the lack of competing economic and employment alternatives. So deterrence operates to stop some fraction of the drugs that begin a journey to the United States. The questions that arise include how much deterrence is present, what aspects of the deterrence effort are most effective, and what steps smugglers take to reduce the risks of losing their payload, being captured, and being punished. Those questions provide part of the framework for the current study. The body of literature suggests that these questions would best be answered by the individuals who are the targets of interventions and are not deterred.

As these studies also point out, understanding the context in which an intervention is expected to be effective is important. Therefore, our study is also devoted to understanding the nature of smuggling networks, the methods used to transport drugs into the United States, and the roles of various players in the process. This information helps interpret individual perceptions of risk, the way smuggling operations are organized to mitigate risk, and the way an individual's role in the operation influences the degree of responsibility or decision-making authority that person has over the operation.

It seems remarkable that there have been so few studies of drug smuggling and drug smuggling interdiction efforts. Drug interdiction is regarded as a key to U.S. foreign policy and national security. It is also a huge expense for federal, state, and local governments.

This book builds on previous work to examine the issue of drug smuggling deterrence from the perspective of convicted drug smugglers housed in federal prisons. This is important for several reasons. The problem of drug use in the United States continues to be important. The demand for illegal drugs remains at extremely high levels, as high as the demand in any other nation in the world. As noted above, interdiction is a costly enterprise, and information that could more effectively deploy personnel or assets would be useful in more efficiently using resources. Lastly, the information from this study should also help inform the overall drug strategy, as it should shed light on one of the least understood, yet most important aspects of the illegal drug business—smuggling.

2 Organization of the Study

A primary goal of this book is to examine the effect of interdiction and other drug enforcement activities on drug smuggling. The objective of the interview component of our work was to gather information on perceptions of the relationship between interdiction operations in the drug source, transit, and arrival zones and the corresponding effect on illegal drug smuggling from individuals with personal experience of smuggling drugs into the United States. The interviews were designed to collect information on how high-level smugglers assess risk, what they perceive as risks, and how these perceptions vary according to their role in the offense. The sample was selected to provide the best answers to these questions, focusing on smugglers with documented histories of smuggling operations who played a decision-making role in the offense that led to conviction. In short, we wanted a sample of smugglers who had multiple successful and unsuccessful attempts at drug smuggling and who were involved in smuggling large quantities of product. Below we describe the study design, providing specific details in Appendix 2.

Study Design

There were two primary goals of this study. The first was to collect information on drug smuggler organizations, transportation methods, and smuggler roles as background to understanding how sample subjects perceived and managed the risks associated with smuggling drugs. The second was to explore points at which a smuggler may have been deterred from smuggling drugs into the United States.

In an effort to build on previous work, the study was designed to collect information from a confined population with direct experience of smuggling drugs into the United States. To maximize the utility of this information, we utilized sample selection procedures that identified individuals rather than institutions, established an interview environment that promoted honesty, included a range of and especially high-level security institutions, used a translator when needed, and recorded and transcribed interviews. We interviewed prisoners in federal facilities because of the likelihood of finding more high-level smugglers in such facilities. Indeed, as Sevigny and Caulkins (2004) found, there are very few high-level smugglers ("kingpins") in state facilities, and federal prisoners are more likely to be part of organized groups of smugglers, to smuggle larger quantities of illegal drugs, and to participate in higher-level roles.

Developing the Questionnaire

Interviews with persons convicted of trafficking drugs into the United States were used to examine the process of drug smuggling. As has been demonstrated, personal interviews with high-level drug smugglers are important sources of information for learning about drug smuggling processes, especially the perception and management of risks.

A questionnaire was designed to conduct a semi-structured, open-ended personal interview. The development of the questionnaire was based on a variety of sources of information. First, several interviews were conducted with U.S. Customs (USCS) agents who had worked undercover narcotics cases in the preceding twenty-four months.[1] Second, the interviews were preceded by an extensive tour by the authors of U.S. Coast Guard and U.S. Customs operations in Miami.[2] Finally, the extant literature was reviewed, focusing on studies relying on personal interviews of inmates (Rockwell International, 1989; Reuter and Haaga, 1989; Wright and Decker, 1994).

The final questionnaire (see Appendix 1) examined a variety of topics, including prior arrests and convictions; the specifics of the inmate's first, most recent, and typical smuggling offenses; and perceptions of the risk associated with smuggling drugs into the United States. After reviewing methods employed by Rockwell International (1989) to measure deterrence, questions measuring the smuggler's reaction to various levels of risk of apprehension, conviction, and sentence were simplified so that the smugglers would not have to make complicated calculations. As a semi-structured interview, the wording, order, and follow-up questions were dependent on the inmate's responses. The instrument was translated into Spanish, and a Spanish-speaking translator was used with inmates who were more comfortable discussing their smuggling activities in Spanish. All interviews were tape-recorded, subject to respondent agreement.

Sample Selection

Given the type of information we sought, we developed sample selection procedures to identify high-level drug smugglers. We were interested in individuals who trafficked large amounts of illicit drugs on a frequent basis; not one-time, low-level street dealers. We believed that these individuals would be more likely to have experience assessing the risks of transporting drugs into the United States. The specific steps in the sample selection process are summarized in Table 2.1.

TABLE 2.1 SAMPLE SELECTION PROCESS

415 cases in original sample
Review of 297 presentence reports to make interviewing decisions
Select 173 for interviewing
135 of 173 located in federal prisons
Approach 73 for participation
Interview 34 drug traffickers

Sample selection began with the identification of all individuals sentenced between 1992 and 1998 who were serving time for a violation of section 18 U.S.C. 2D1.1 of the U.S. Criminal Code. This section refers to unlawful manufacturing, importing, exporting, and trafficking of illegal drugs (including possession with the intent to commit these offenses and attempt or conspiracy). The time frame was limited to offenders sentenced since 1992 because that was the first year the Bureau of Prisons began distinguishing between crack and powder cocaine. The 1992 guidelines also provided for the imposition of penalties for "conspiracy" to import cocaine.[3] The year 1998 was the cutoff because data from that year were the most recent available. The U.S. Sentencing Commission (USSC) provided data that included demographic and sentencing information for all offenders sentenced from 1992 through 1998 for drug trafficking as either the primary or one of the five most serious charges. Four hundred fifteen cases met these criteria.

The USSC data for all 415 cases were reviewed to identify high-level drug smugglers. Based on the literature, our interviews with undercover agents, and interviews with U.S. Customs Service officials, variables we thought would distinguish between high- and low-level smugglers included aggravated role in the offense, criminal history, offense level, acceptance of responsibility, and whether the defendant provided substantial assistance to the government. To explore how these variables might be used to select potential interviewees, we asked the Monitoring Division of the Sentencing Commission to provide a sample of presentence reports (PSR).

Presentence reports are generated by probation officers for judicial consideration at sentencing. A typical PSR includes demographic information; information on the instant and related offenses (obtained from codefendants, undercover agents, or confidential informants); criminal history; family, medical, and employment history; and a computation of the adjusted offense level (which includes adjustments for the role in the offense, acceptance of responsibility, etc.). The files also include copies of the indictment, the plea agreement, objections by the prosecutor or the government, and the sentencing report.

Using the detailed information in the sample of PSRs and comparing that information against data available on those cases, three criteria were used to identify 118 individuals with little decision-making authority in the known offenses who were, therefore, not important to the study.[4]

The Sentencing Commission was asked to provide PSRs for the remaining sample of 297 cases, of which 286 were reviewed.[5] Although the levels of detail in PSRs varied across reports, a specific set of elements was used to make a determination of the offender's level of involvement in drug smuggling and to determine whether we wanted to interview the offender. Based on this review, 174 cases were identified as potential interview candidates, of which 78 percent or 135 individuals were identified by the Bureau of Prisons as currently being housed in a federal institution.[6]

We reviewed the final 135 cases based on the prisoners' availability in common facilities. Specifically, we were interested in interviewing prisoners in prisons that held at least 6 prisoners who met our selection criteria. This resulted in a final sample of 81 drug smugglers located in seventeen different federal prisons. They were among the most heavily involved drug smugglers of all prisoners in the U.S. federal penal system.

Interview Sample

Although eighty-one smugglers were originally identified as being located at the selected institutions, only seventy-three were approached for interviews.[7] Of them, thirty-four agreed to participate—a 52 percent refusal rate. Most of those who refused did not want to help (56 percent), while the others had lawyers who advised them not to participate (16 percent), felt they had nothing to share because they were innocent (11 percent), did not want to relive the past (5 percent), did not believe it would benefit them personally (5 percent), were appealing their convictions (5 percent), and had language barriers (3 percent). When the interviewed group was compared with the seventy-three prisoners approached, we found the two groups to be similar on some of the most important indicators of the offenders' participation in the offenses: offense level and role in the offense.

A description of the final sample of thirty-four individuals who were interviewed is included in Table 2.2. This table provides the salient descriptive characteristics of individuals (role, citizenship, age) and information about their smuggling history (country of origin, role, criminal history points, sentence length). The majority of people in the sample were U.S. citizens (sixteen), though many of the citizens were born in Cuba. Colombians made up the second largest nationality (seven). All the smugglers operated in the Caribbean as a point of origin, and with a single exception, their destination point was the United States.

Nine of the smugglers were arrested in 1991, with the balance of arrests distributed across the years 1989–1997. Eleven smugglers were in their forties, and eight were in their fifties. In all, this was a somewhat older sample than we had expected, but it reinforces the prisoners' long-standing involvement in drug smuggling enterprises. Seven smugglers received life sentences.

TABLE 2.2   DEMOGRAPHIC CHARACTERISTICS OF THE SAMPLE

	N = 34	Percentage
Gender		
Male	34	100
Age at Sentencing		
Between 26 and 30	5	15
Between 31 and 40	10	29
Between 41 and 50	11	32
Greater than 50	8	24
Race		
White	31	91
Black	2	6
Other and Missing	1	3
Hispanic Origin		
Non-Hispanic	5	15
Hispanic	29	85
Citizenship		
U.S. Citizen	16	47
Legal Alien/Resident	10	29
Illegal Alien	5	15
Unknown Status/Missing	3	9
Country of Origin		
Cuba	10	29
Colombia	7	21
United States	6	18
Puerto Rico	3	9
Venezuela	2	6
Bahamas	1	3
Haiti	1	3
Peru	1	3
Unknown	3	9
Offense Level		
32–37	5	15
38–40	10	29
41–43	17	50
44–49	2	6

TABLE 2.2   (Continued)

	N = 34	Percentage
Role Offense		
Manager, Organizer, Supervisor, or Leader	5	15
Manager or Supervisor >5 Participants	10	29
Leader or Organizer >5 Participants	19	56
Criminal History Points		
0	19	56
1 through 3	6	18
4 through 6	7	21
7 through 10	0	0
>10	2	6
Months Sentenced to Prison		
60 Months or Less	2	6
61–180 Months	0	0
181–240 Months	11	32
241–360 Months	12	35
Greater than 360 Months	9	26

The shortest sentence was eight years, and eleven individuals received sentences of more than twenty-five years. The offense levels for which they were convicted also reinforce the depth of involvement in smuggling on the part of members of our sample.

Although the PSRs categorize each smuggler as having played a specific role in the offense, smugglers were asked to describe their most substantial roles in the drug smuggling operations they had been involved in. Table 2.3 confirms that the majority of the smugglers had some management responsibility over the operations. Five were brokers, individuals who negotiated between Colombian sources and U.S. buyers to organize loads of cocaine to be smuggled from Colombia. Fourteen described themselves as transportation managers, managing transportation crews, and two described themselves as managers of operations, the people running the whole operation. These roles represent the most significant high-level roles in the smuggling process. Eight members of the sample played roles in the actual transportation of the

TABLE 2.3   MOST SUBSTANTIAL ROLE IN CURRENT OFFENSE

Most Substantial Role	Number of Prisoners	Percentage
Transportation Manager	14	40
Manager of Operations	2	6
Transporter	6	18
Broker	5	15
Money Launderer	2	6
Receiver/Offloader	2	6
Did Not Admit to Any Specific Roles	3	9

drugs, with six describing themselves as "transporters" (e.g., boat captains and crew members) and two as offloaders responsible for the removal and receipt of the drugs.

There is also diversity in the method of smuggling (see Table 2.4), with the primary method being through the use of a private seagoing vessel (62 percent). Nine individuals used private planes to make air drops, usually in mid-shipment locations, and eight used commercial airplanes as their method of smuggling.

The smugglers reflected a deep and long-standing involvement in drug smuggling. Table 2.5 describes each subject's history of involvement in smuggling drugs into the United States. More than half the sample admitted to being involved in ten or more smuggling events, with 40 percent of those in more than fifty events. However, although the sample included a substantial number of experienced smugglers, it also included a number (40 percent) who admitted to less experience.

TABLE 2.4   METHOD OF TRANSPORT OF DRUGS FOR
CONVICTION OFFENSE

Methods Described in PSR	Number of Prisoners	Percentage*
Commercial Air	6	18
Commercial Vessel	8	24
Private Air	9	26
Private Vessel	21	62
Other	1	3

*Percentages do not equal 100, because some PSRs indicated experience with more than one method.

TABLE 2.5   LIFETIME SMUGGLING EVENTS

Number of Lifetime Smuggling Events	Number of Prisoners	Percentage
More than 50	7	20
10–49	11	32
2–9	1	3
1	9	26
More than 1, but Unspecified	3	9
0	3	9

As evidence of the rich histories of the smugglers, following are brief characterizations of some members of the sample.

Subject A: A forty-year-old Venezuelan whose first smuggling trip took place in 1979 and last in 1988. He estimated that he made more than fifty trips as transportation manager, smuggling four hundred to five hundred kilograms of cocaine using vessels and airplanes between Colombia and Miami and between Colombia and Tampa, Florida.

Subject B: A forty-eight-year-old Cuban whose first major drug smuggling trip took place in 1988 and last in 1995. He refused to identify the number of trips he made, but did say that his role was as transportation manager transporting seven hundred to eight hundred kilograms by private vessel from the Bahamas to Florida and a thousand to fifteen hundred kilograms from Puerto Rico to Florida.

Subject C: A forty-three-year-old Cuban who began smuggling drugs into the United States in 1976 and was caught in 1993. He claimed to have made more than fifty trips, and his primary responsibility was constructing hidden compartments on private vessels and serving as boat captain, moving more than five hundred kilograms from Colombia to the Bahamas to Miami.

Subject D: A fifty-five-year-old Cuban who began smuggling drugs using commercial vessels in 1975 and was caught in 1991. He claimed to have made forty to fifty trips, organizing the movement of large loads of cocaine shipments from Colombia to Miami in containers.

Subject E: A forty-year-old Colombian who admitted to organizing one shipment of three thousand kilograms of cocaine using a commercial vessel traveling from Colombia to Philadelphia in 1991.

Based on comparisons of the interviewed group and the original sample, the groups located in federal prison, and those approached, the researchers felt that the sampling process achieved its goals. We intended to interview a sample of individuals who could tell us, in detail, about the process and risks in smuggling drugs. To that end, we wanted to include high-level smugglers with considerable experience. We succeeded in doing so by a number of measures. The final sample was more involved in smuggling, convicted of higher-level offenses, had more years in the smuggling business, and had a larger role in smuggling than any of the subgroups we considered for inclusion in the sample. Further, the characteristics of those who refused to be interviewed were largely similar to the characteristics of those we did interview.

We also had confidence in the veracity of the information provided by our subjects. Although answers relating to particularly sensitive and potentially incriminating acts should be viewed with some degree of discretion, the vast majority of interviewees were forthcoming, and responses rarely contradicted information provided on the PSRs. For example, 94 percent of the subjects' criminal history responses during interviews were consistent with those indicated on the PSRs. Most of the demographic information was consistent, and only 24 percent of the interviewees described their roles in the offense as being less than that indicated in the PSR.[8]

Summary

A thoughtful selection process successfully identified some of the highest-level drug smugglers in federal prison at the time of our study. Access to the PSRs proved invaluable in both the selection of the sample and as preparation for the interviews. As a result, interviewers were able to begin the interviews with some familiarity with the individuals and their roles in drug smuggling events, which also allowed them to assess the veracity of the information being provided during the interviews.

The thirty-four drug smugglers in the final sample were heavily involved in drug smuggling. Indeed, they represented the deepest end among those confined in terms of their sentences, roles, responsibilities, and offense levels. The majority described their roles as being responsible for multiple aspects of the operation, for all aspects of the transport, or for a particular aspect of the actual transport, all of which required detailed knowledge of and personal responsibility for the transport of the drugs into the United States. More than half also admitted to being involved in at least ten smuggling operations, with a number indicating involvement in more than fifty. Their experiences enabled interviewers to collect in-depth information on how smuggler operations are organized, risks associated with different roles, and strategies used to minimize and reduce risks.

Care was taken to encourage the collection of valuable information by working with federal prison officials to identify acceptable call-out procedures (procedures that would not cause suspicion among the subjects or fellow prisoners) and interview locations. Subjects were allowed to refuse interviews and to answer only certain questions. Conversations were tape-recorded, and a translator was used when needed.

The success of our selection process enabled us to collect useful information in all interest areas. Although the focus of the study was on how smugglers assessed risk, the next three chapters begin by providing a context for interpreting these assessments.

We use extensive quotations to describe smuggling operations, the methods used to transport drugs, and the various roles required to transport drugs into the United States. Understanding the characteristics of smuggling operations is critical to interpreting what we learned about risk. To fully appreciate smuggler responses to questions about risk, it is necessary to understand how their roles in particular smuggling events shaped the degree of decision-making authority and consequently the way they perceived and minimized risk.

3 Drug Smuggling Organizations

lthough the interviews were not focused on describing smuggling organizations, it was impossible to avoid the subject in conversations about how loads were organized, who owned the drugs, and how information was communicated across groups. Many of the smugglers also had long histories of smuggling drugs and were therefore able to discuss changes in smuggling organizations over the past twenty years. It is from these discussions that we are able to describe the structure of smuggling organizations and how drugs are moved from the source country to the United States.

As we began talking to smugglers about smuggling organizations, we began to hear such terms as *office* and *broker*. We used these terms during the interviews so that we could better understand descriptions of the smuggling enterprise. In some cases, the smugglers seemed to be unclear about how their contacts in Colombia fit into the smuggling organizations, but in other cases, the smugglers knew how loads were arranged and how things were organized. Most often, these smugglers were Colombian or had managed the transportation of drugs for so many years that they had grown to understand how their contacts in Colombia operated. We relied on the descriptions of these two groups to describe the structure of drug smuggling organizations in Colombia during the late 1980s and the 1990s.

Movement Away from Cartels

Past research has shown that the structure of drug organizations in Colombia has evolved over the past twenty years (DEA, 1997; Bunker and Sullivan, 1998). Drug distribution groups in Colombia became formal organizations under the leaders of the Medellin cartel. These organizations operated in much the same way as traditional formal organizations, with a chief executive officer responsible for executive officers who were in charge of separate functions of the organization. Because this organization was hierarchical and the leaders controlled the movement of drugs through the organization, their deaths and increased Colombian and U.S. law enforcement pressure led first to fragmentation and ultimately to the demise of the Medellin cartel.

The Medellin cartel was quickly replaced by the Cali cartel, a loose association of five major drug syndicates, each representing different aspects of the business. In this organization, a strict top-down command and control structure was the norm, exercising control over subordinates through fear and intimidation. The Cali cartel ruled the Colombian drug enterprise until the mid-1990s, when two of the leaders were incarcerated, which caused organizational fragmentation into specialized groups. According to the smugglers, smaller groups were now able to coordinate movement of drugs into the United States without control by the cartel. It is interesting to speculate about the impact of each organizational structure—highly organized or loosely confederated—on successful smuggling.

Many of the smugglers in our sample had smuggled drugs since the 1970s and 1980s, and they told us about the shift in structure away from cartels and into less organized groups. In many cases, the current structure may be likened to the networks described by Williams (1998: 155) as a series of connected nodes (individuals or organizations) with both a core and periphery networks with significant linkages among them. Linkages with the core are based on relationships and trust, while the weaker links to the periphery are based on function.

The smugglers in our sample confirmed the impact of the removal of the heads of the Cali cartel on the organization and the subsequent splintering of the organization into functional units. The result was a shift from a centralized operation controlled by a few to a number of networks operating individually and as a group to move drugs out of Colombia. A few of the smugglers described this shift in the following ways.

> It's more spread out now. Ever since all those major groups had either been arrested or turned themselves in or retired . . . but when a group like that—they say when the Ochoas went in to turn themselves in, all those employees they had, all those people that worked for them, they knew what they were doing . . . they had the gift of all these connection. So what happened? It all spread around. (221)[1]

> Well, it is different—it's smaller groups now. Like before it was all cartel. It was a group of gentlemen, that, you know, it was like a board. We make decisions together and stuff. Now it is all broken up, but, you know, the drugs are still coming in. Even more than ever. (1)

After the cartels broke up, many groups shared control over movement of drugs as the market readjusted to the change in control.

> It all spread around. It was worse because in the beginning there is an organization. There's people being organized. Now you got people everywhere, you know? And it doesn't mean that's going to generate seven hundred kilos for every little person that is left. No, these people—this one might deal with ten and the other ten. (22)

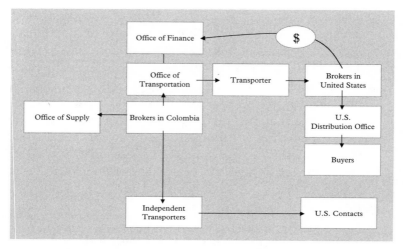

Figure 3.1   The Structure of Drug Smuggling Organizations

The smugglers were consistent in their characterization of the current structure as two-tiered networks made up of core and periphery members. The core, described to us as *offices*, used brokers and transporters to generate loads and move them to the United States and to return the profit to Colombian sources. One office may have multiple brokers in Colombia and the United States, just as it had multiple transportation groups. The brokers allow the offices to function independently, typically in isolation from one another. The connection between the offices and brokers and how they connect to move drugs to the United States and profits back to Colombia is depicted in Figure 3.1.

Structure and Movement of Drugs

In this section, we use the information from the smugglers about the structure of smuggling operations to describe how the different groups organize loads and transport them to the United States.

Suppliers

Many of the smugglers in our sample were not that familiar with how coca farmers fit in the business. Many were familiar with the fact that the coca crops were located in Peru and that the paste was developed there. One mentioned that the Colombians were planting coca crops of their own. The smugglers also felt that either the farmers or someone the farmers worked for sold the paste to Colombian labs to be processed into cocaine. What remained elusive to them was how the product was moved from the farm to the lab and who was in control of that movement.

> A guy, a peasant in Colombia, if he grows oranges, he can't sell the oranges because they rot, you know. So, if he grows bananas, he can't sell them, right? But if somebody comes and asks him, you know, "Can you grow some coca leaves for us, and we pay you for whatever you produce," well the guy is going to do it. So why don't you pay $5 for each orange that this guy produce[s]? He doesn't care what it is, what he's growing. Because the trafficker is not, is not growing the coke. It's some guy in the jungle doing that. (13)

One smuggler mentioned that organizing a load of drugs for transport was not as simple as it might appear. There were a series of payoffs. The farmer was paid off by the chemist, who was paid off by the broker, who was paid off by the office. It was also necessary to pay for transport from Peru to Colombia and to spend money for protection from law enforcement or guerillas. When working independently, this process was even less organized because the person attempting to generate a load must initiate each payoff individually. Generally, the identities of the players and the process involved in this aspect of the smuggling operation were unclear to the smugglers, except that they knew that the coca was purchased from farmers and either processed independently and sold through a broker or bought and processed by the office.

> The farmer goes and contacts an individual and says, "Look, I have—I processed this. Would you buy it from me?" He has the money [and] says, "Okay, I'll buy it from you." So this guy goes and he contacts a broker from one of the offices. He says, "Look I have to send this to the United States." (13)

Although members of our sample may have been unclear about how drugs were grown and processed in Colombia, none of them mentioned any problems about finding large quantities of drugs to move or loads that needed to be transported. One smuggler mentioned that it was as easy to get cocaine in Colombia as it was to get coffee.

> I go down there [Colombia] to try to find somebody that wants to put cocaine into the country [United States], and the place is teeming with people that are drowning in cocaine, looking for any way to get rid of it. (24)

The identity of the person who actually owns the load or was paying the farmer or the chemist was difficult for smugglers to understand as well; however, it was clear that one emerging trend was for multiple owners to ship larger loads, often more than five hundred kilos. Some smugglers referred to people who had the drugs in their possession in Colombia as the owners or did not actually know who the owners were, except that they were Colombians. Smugglers with a better understanding of the structure in Colombia described getting the drugs from either a broker or the office in charge of transportation in Colombia, but they identified the owner as having sold the drugs to the broker or office to move them into the United States. One of the smugglers in the sample who performed the function of broker indicated that he purchased loads from multiple people in Colombia. He reiterated the fact that accessing drugs is not difficult and pointed out that it is done through recommendations from others in the business, underscoring the nature of small networks.

> This [owning drugs] is something that you can not hide in Colombia. (15)

Brokers in Colombia

After the cartels broke up, the brokers became the leaders of the wholesale trafficking business because they had the contacts, underscoring the key roles that relationships and contacts played in the business. A number of large brokers operated in Colombia, in contrast to the cartel days when there were only a small number. Brokers linked the farmers, chemists, owners, and offices and facilitated the movement of drugs. The links between these groups were usually based on trust and family ties, and brokers worked with one or more smuggling groups to move loads.

> After commissioning a farmer to grow coca leaves and after harvesting it, then they [the person asking the farmer to grow coca leaves] sell it to a broker, and the broker sells it to the guys in the lab, and the guys in the lab produce the kilos, and then he [the broker] goes into the city and finds a buyer. "I've got so many kilos. Would you like to buy it?" (13)

> So, this person in Colombia contacts the office, has fifty kilos [bought from farmer] and they go to a broker. So he [the broker] makes a contact to one of the offices. (13)

Brokers may also serve a number of vital functions in a smuggling event. For example, they may assist in the negotiations between the office and owner on price, or they may be the contact for an office on the transportation or distribution in the United States. Offices may use many brokers to fill these and other positions.

A primary function of the broker was to organize the load or put the load together. By this we mean to suggest that brokers combine several different suppliers' drugs into a complete shipment. The broker may work independently—that is, may move the load himself—or may put a load together for sale to the office in charge of transportation. Brokers generally found as many owners as they needed to generate the size of the load appropriate for the planned method of transport.

> [Y]ou have a collector, and . . . a bunch of people will invest in the load. It's like selling shares of stock. This person will put up this amount of money. Another person will put up another amount of money, and they in effect maybe own two or three keys. Then the collector, or whatever, whatever you want to call him, puts all this together, and this joint venture goes on a plane. So a proprietary interest in this was really shared by many. (24)

When asked why it was done this way, the smuggler replied:

> I imagine it's—well, it's a way of raising capital. I would imagine the same reason a corporation has shares—sells shares of stock. If you're down there and you're going to put something together, you don't have capital. You sell shares, you know, and it's even insured. (24)

It may have also been a way to protect against combined loss. For instance, if a load of fifteen hundred kilos was spread across three transportation routes, the likelihood of one-third to two-thirds of the load reaching the United States was enhanced. One owner was likely to prefer part getting through to nothing at all.

> They figured five hundred kilos, although that is a lot of money here, it's not much money down there, and they could absorb that loss. (5)

Some brokers worked independently. For example, one transporter worked for a broker whom he described in the following manner.

> He didn't work for anyone. He worked on commission and he trusted me. I never met the guys from Medellin, or anybody. This guy wasn't the owner of the drugs; he was the owner of the land strip. But they trusted him and he trusted me. He needed the owners of the drugs because he wanted them to use his land strip and he offered them the transportation that I had. (3)

These independent brokers may put together a load that includes some drugs for the broker and some for the transporter, creating a small organization made up of the broker, the transporter, and the contact in the United States.

What the independent brokers gained in profit and independence, they lost in security and the potential ability to move large loads of drugs into the United States. Because they did not have the contacts that were available to larger organizations, they had to be more responsive to smaller suppliers, a characteristic that reinforced the nature of short networks in such distribution systems.

Identifying the number of independents as compared to those working through offices was difficult and may require additional research. Many of the smugglers in the sample were unclear about the role of their contacts in Colombia and may have misunderstood the relationships. Additionally, what the brokers made out of the deal beyond a small profit for negotiating the load was unclear.

Offices

Our subjects reported that after the cartels broke up, organizations were made up of networks with small offices, each with fifty to a hundred people who carried out the functions of the office. The load was obtained through the office, which is the center for moving the drugs. The office organized the specific aspects of the operation and was the connection between the brokers and the transporters. There were a number of offices associated with each primary task involved in a drug smuggling offense, including offices in charge of supply and packaging, transportation, distribution, and money.

The offices in Colombia had brokers who connected the farmers to the lab and the lab to the offices. The brokers supplied the drugs to the supply offices, and the supply office worked with the transportation office on packaging. At the same time, the transportation office was negotiating the price with the transportation manager and the broker in the United States. The transportation office also worked with the broker in the United States, the office in charge of distribution, and the office in charge of money to negotiate profit and a method of getting money back from the United States. Multiple offices may put together a load, or one office may have multiple owners moving one load. The number of owners involved in a load was also a function of the size of the load.

> If a person wants to send coke to the U.S., he has to buy the merchandise from the office, for say $3,500 or $2,000 a kilo and then they have to give the transporter the merchandise to be transported. The office does nothing but has all the power. When they reach the four hundred, that's a load. The transporter charges the office $1,500 a kilo and the people who want to ship it, $2,000; this is payment for using the office's name and airstrip. (29)

By breaking the organization into offices, functional responsibilities were limited, and the flow of drugs into the United States was separate from the flow of money out of the United States. This is an important aspect of the distribution network and illustrates the insularity of many of the processes of drug smuggling. If one group is infiltrated, the others are protected.

> They [Colombians] got connections all over the United States, people who do the smuggling, people who do the selling, people who launder money, people who take care of the money. You know, they buy and sell what they call offices. A guy got five offices. One office takes care of this. The other office takes care of different things. They tried not to put the money with the drugs. That way—before, they used to do. Now they don't. They got lots of, you know—smarter. The guy who picked up the money don't have nothing to do with the guy who's bringing it in. That way, if you get caught, you cannot tell on the guy with the money, and the guy with the money cannot tell on the guy with the drugs. All the offices go to one place, Colombia. Say, I got my office. You the head of that office. You know me, but the people working with you don't know that I am the boss. That way they cannot get to me. (32)

One office worked with the brokers or directly with the labs to put together a load. Another office for transportation may have different groups organizing different parts of the transport—to midpoint, at midpoint, from midpoint to the United States. The managers of each of the operations may have known the contact in Colombia, but they do not know each other. The offices were also known by the routes they controlled and, consequently, the transportation groups that worked for them.

> It's like you live in Brooklyn, and you know who is, who is the, Jew who lends money. You know who is—you know everybody in the neighborhood. That you want to associate with them is one thing, but you know what is going on in there. You know who has got the hot items for sale and who has got the carjacking stuff and, you know, goods and everything are stolen goods. You know everything if you are a

street guy. Well, in Colombia, these individuals are known to be narco-traffickers or whatever, but they have a route. It's called a route. So they have an office, and they have scouts looking for merchandise. (13)

So despite the money involved, despite the cultural issues, the distribution network was characterized by an informal nature. One smuggler described the function of the office in the following way.

When you get there, the first thing you see when you come in, it says no gambling, no drinking. Then you go in there and there is pool tables. People are sitting around and talking, and then there's a blackboard with arrivals and departures, and it says like . . . Brothers leaving the twentieth, half a load, have space for four hundred kilos, and then, you know, anybody would come in and stake out what they want to send. (29)

The office in charge of the operation (that makes the deal between the broker and the seller) offered insurance. The negotiations that took place were described by one smuggler in the following way.

The farmer goes and contacts an individual and says, "Look, I have—I processed this. Would you buy it from me?" The guy has the money says, "Okay, I'll buy it from you." So this guy goes and he contacts a broker from one of those offices. He says, "Look, I have to send this to the United States." He [the broker] says, "Yeah, we have space. So, do you want insurance or not?" And I say, "Well, how much is insurance?" "Well the insurance is $2,000." (13)

The office provided insurance to the broker at a rate per kilo. If the merchandise was confiscated, the broker and eventually the customer got paid the actual value of the merchandise in Colombia.

If the load was successful, the U.S. broker gave the money to the office in Colombia, who gave it to the broker, who gave it to the person who invested the money.

The office also negotiated the price for transportation with the owner, through the broker.

> So, this guy in the office says, "I charge for the transportation of the kilo. I charge $7,000." Plus or minus insurance. So it's for the guy to accept. The owner of the merchandise is to accept whether he pays that much money for the transportation because he probably knows that the price in the market right here is $14,000. So he says, "I'm paying $8,000 for the insurance, and I make $4,000 per kilo." (13)

Price is impacted by the transportation cost, which is a function of time, money, and risk of the route and method. The owners choose certain offices based on their routes. Some routes may be more expensive but quicker. Others may be cheap but take six months.

One of the smugglers in our sample worked for the office as a broker, not as a transporter. He brokered between people in Miami looking for drugs and his contacts in Colombia, and he was sent to Miami when loads were arriving to oversee operations and handle anything that went wrong.

Transporters

Most of the drug smugglers in our sample could be described as transporters or managers of the transport. Every load transported into the United States was organized by a group of people, of whom one was in charge of transportation (which may include transportation from a mid-shipment location); one was in charge of distribution; and one was in charge of the money. Transportation groups may work for an organization or a contact in Colombia or may be independent and work through recommendations either in the country of origin or the destination. Most independent transporters worked either alone or with a small group and rarely handle more than the transport from point A to point B. On the other hand, transportation groups working for individuals in Colombia were more organized and had contact with members of the group working in Colombia and the United States.

Transportation managers were hired by the office or brokers in Colombia to organize and complete the transport between point A and point B. For all the transporters in our sample, point B was the United States. Managers were called by the office or broker and told, for example, that a load going from Colombia to the Bahamas needed to be brought into the Florida Keys. Before calling, the organization knew the transportation specialties of the manager and his group and contacted the manager based on the specifications he provided. Some managers described negotiating with Colombia about the transshipment location or method of transport, largely driven by their own experiences and capabilities.

It may take as much as a year or as little as a few weeks to organize an operation. In general, though, organizing a load takes a significant amount of planning. First everyone had to be organized; the merchandise had to be set up; the price had to be negotiated; the logistics of security, the coordinates in Colombia, and a midpoint must be set up; fuel must be arranged; security must be coordinated; transport must be set up from the midpoint; and offloading crews must be set up and a location to offload identified. According to our sources, it took at least two or three people to organize all this at each stop. One smuggler indicated that the toughest part of the operation was deciding what country to move the load through.

> I guess people call it easy money, but it isn't easy. You know, it takes a lot of time—a lot of work. . . . You don't just go down there and say tomorrow I want a job. It requires planning, and then got to get everybody together. (29)

None of the smugglers involved in transportation were able to identify a time when they wanted to smuggle drugs, but there was nothing to smuggle. Those who played less prominent roles in drug smuggling also told us that there were no slow periods; when they were ready to work, the product (cocaine) was present. One smuggler did mention, however, that everyone took a break between Thanksgiving and New Year's Day to avoid being in jail during the holidays.

Many transportation managers reported that the office in charge of transportation or a broker in Colombia hired them. Transportation managers tended to work for the same person or contact for a long time. This was one of the few enduring relationships described to us. Working for one person was common because of the trust that had been established, particularly since the loads were fronted to the transportation team.

The smugglers were varied in terms of the number of methods they had to offer, the routes they used, the extent of the transport they took on, and whether they were responsible for the offload in the United States. Often, this varied based on the method, the size of the load, and the number of people involved in the operation.

> When I would bring in the merchandise, sometimes I only rented the plane. Sometimes the people in Colombia give me the merchandise and say they would pay for the transportation, and sometimes they would say they had the merchandise in Santa Marta but needed transportation, so I rented the plane to them for $1,250 a kilo. (3)

Once hired, the transportation manager was also responsible for hiring a crew or multiple crews. Depending on the aspects of the transport for which he has responsibility, the transporter may be hiring as many as four crews: one to transport from the source to the midpoint, one to deal with the logistics at the transfer location, one to transport from the midpoint to the United States, and one to offload the drugs. As many as ten to fifteen people may be involved at each stage.

Depending on the size of the load, usually only one person brought in the load on a speedboat or a fishing vessel, with maybe two or three people on a large boat like a yacht. The boat crews were usually American or Cuban—people who would fit in with the Florida boating and fishing communities.

> He [his partner] always wanted to use Cuban people to work with him, and I never thought that that was [the] right idea. . . . Cubans are like—you know, they're signaled like drug smugglers. Just like if you say Colombia—you look at Colombians, you're going to think about drugs right away. (22)

Smuggling using commercial boating vessels involved more people and also involved more organization. When flying the drugs in, transportation managers said they relied on one pilot, either an American or Colombian, to fly the plane. But the transportation managers estimated that there were usually six to eight people working each operation, including contacts in Colombia, transporters, and contacts in the United States.

Whether working for the transportation manager as a captain, a pilot, or a crew member, the transporter was asked to move without much notice and was given only latitude and longitude points for the rendezvous. Only the manager had input in the pickup point and other specifics of the operation.

Depending on the agreement between the office in Colombia, the transportation manager, and the broker in the United States, the crew may or may not be involved in the offload and delivery of the merchandise. Some transporters brought a boat into a designated strip; others offloaded drugs into a house; and still others moved it from a warehouse to a rendezvous point. In many cases, even if this were part of the transportation, the same boat crew would not be responsible for this part of the operation because the manager would not want crew members to know where the load was going. In other cases, the manager would not want to be involved in unloading or delivering the merchandise.

None of these people may know each other, or one may know one other person, but usually the manager of each leg of the transport knew the members of his crew and one other person in the transportation scheme in front of and behind him. The crew members knew their contacts only and did not know the next phases of the journey, which is protection for the organizers.

Usually there was no contact with transporters during the smuggling operation, unless by radio or cell phone and only to exchange vital information on problems and connection points. If there was communication, it occurred using coded messages and was between the organizer and the heads of the different offices and then with their transporters. Once the drugs were in the United States, there was typically an arrangement for the transporter to notify his office of his success, again through a coded message. One manager using a combination of his crew and independents described the communication this way.

> They would call me up, tell me where to be, sometimes longitude and latitude, and they tell me when I have to be there. My name having been referred to him as somebody who was very trustworthy and who knew his way around the Bahamas. Once there, I took it to my warehouse and called my boss and said the horse is in the barn. Then they would come and pick it up. (12)

Independent transporters lose some of the benefits associated with working with an organization. For example, they are responsible for their own protection, are not in communication with anyone during the smuggling operation, and are at more risk if something happens to the load. It is more difficult for them to establish the trust that is so important in smuggling.

Costs of Doing Business
Because most of the smugglers we talked to had experience as transportation managers or transporters, we were able to get information on the specific costs associated with transporting

drugs to the United States. Smugglers told us that routes and costs vary by speed, risk, and method, though brokers in Colombia and the United States figure out the best price. The organizer usually told transporters what they could afford and negotiated the load based on that. The price was based on a combination of what was paid in the past, the risk involved, and the market price. Only one smuggler noted that he had once rejected a load because the price was too low.

In most cases, smugglers indicated that they were paid approximately 50 percent of the load to organize the transport. Two payment options were presented to them. One was to keep a proportion of the load (usually between 50 and 70 percent) that covered the payment that had been negotiated and then some as a security measure (sometimes as much as 20 percent). The smuggler would hold it until the distributor came back and exchanged the load for cash. The other option was to sell the drugs themselves. The first option involved less risk for the transporter, but some preferred the second option because they could make more if they sold the drugs for a good price. Transporters paid for crew and expenses associated with transport out of this fee.

Holding 50 to 70 percent was considered insurance. One smuggler noted that this was a more recent phenomenon that has evolved since the demise of cartels because the loads were being broken up and given to multiple distributors and on to other sellers. One of the transporters described the following decision-making process.

It depends on the circumstances of the people that would sell it to me, the manner they had. Where they had a good demand and I didn't feel safe to sell it to them, I would make the arrangements with the Colombians and get the money instead. And, of course, there was also a margin of profit. It depends on the price that I would have entered with Colombians on the merchandise. There would always be a margin of profit which would pay for the expenses. (16)

Owners of the routes or transporters negotiated the price per kilo with the office, which then negotiated with the owner either directly or through a broker. One organizer told us that if the

> street value is $14,000, then try to negotiate $11,000 or $12,000 for transport, but $14,000 was not all that was made per kilo because [the buyer] may be selling to the end user for $20,000. (16)

Payment for organizing the load has stayed the same for a few years and has varied based on the price on the street only. If the Colombian contacts decided to hold the load or use a different method, the organizer of the transport would get a proportion of what he was originally going to be paid for expenses incurred.

Often, there was also a charge for holding a proportion of the load beyond the specified number of days (seven to ten days) in the form of rent. According to the smugglers, the rent came to approximately $2,000 a day or $200 per kilo. At least one smuggler said that the role of transporter is the best because it pays the most, although this role also involves the highest levels of risk.

> When I reach the four hundred, then that's the load, and it's a bunch of people involved. When it gets here, all I got is a beeper number and you call him. I say, you know, "It's here. Come pick it up." If you got like, they say, a hundred kilos, I will give you fifty kilos, I say "Here is fifty kilos. You got twenty-four hours to bring me my money. In twenty-four hours, you don't bring my money, I start charging rent, $200 rent a day per kilo." So you know, you move it out. (29)

Some of the smugglers discussed the payments made to crew members and others involved in the offense. The charge for transportation was always a per-kilo cost and did not vary significantly.

On the other hand, payment was based on the individual's role in the offense. Following are some examples.

- A transporter charged the office $1,500 a kilo, and the office charged the people who wanted to ship it $2,000 to use their name and landing strip.
- A boat captain was paid $250,000 to drive a boat from the Bahamas to Florida.
- A transportation manager charged $2,000 a kilo and paid captains $250,000.
- Captains bringing in marijuana were paid less because cocaine involves more profit and a longer sentence.
- A transporter paid a couple of million dollars to move 3,000 kilos in a compartment of a commercial freighter.
- A captain paid $1 million to move 400 kilos in the compartment of a sailboat.
- An offloader was paid $150,000 to unload 2,200 kilos.
- Pilots were paid $3,000 per kilo.
- An accountant helping to organize a load made $40,000.
- Boat captains were paid 30 to 40 percent of the load by one manager.

Losing a Load

Because most of the smugglers we interviewed were either transporters or managers of the transport, they were familiar with the repercussions of losing the load. The manager of the transport and his transporters were responsible if the load was lost while it was in their possession. For example, if the manager is organizing movement of the load from the Bahamas to Miami and the boat captain was being chased and throws the load overboard, the transporter and the manager of that leg of the operation were responsible.

The responsibility does, however, depend on how the load was lost. If the load was seized by law enforcement, the transporter would have to prove that it was seized, often through the newspapers, and the loss would not be considered an acceptable loss. If the transporter could prove that the load was seized by law enforcement or if the newspapers did not report the full load,[2] the transporter would offer to do another load for free or at a reduced rate. If the Colombian source trusted the transporter, the source might accept this offer. If the transporter was not trusted, an investigation would ensue, and if the transporter's claim was not proven, the transporter would have to pay for all the load or only the part allegedly taken by the police. If the load was lost to law enforcement, everyone would lose. The organizer of the transport would lose the most because he may also have to take care of his crew and their battle with the legal system.

Losing part of the load during a transport was not acceptable unless a plane was air-dropping bales to a boat. This type of transfer is more likely to result in lost bales, which is why many smugglers preferred to land the plane. If some bales were lost during the airdrop, either the transporter or the pilot would have to pay the Colombians, depending on who was deemed responsible (for example, if the pilot was flying too high, causing bales to break on impact with the ocean or to miss the drop zone).

If a boat was being chased by law enforcement, the crew was told to turn around and try to make it back to port because it takes too long to dump bales and the bales would have to be broken up so that they would not float. This way both the merchandise and the crew are saved. One smuggler mentioned that he would dump the drugs only if he were absolutely sure of being caught because the cost of paying for the load is much higher than the cost of a potential encounter with U.S. law enforcement.

One smuggler mentioned the following about assessing who was wrong and the potential harm that may come to that person.

There's a lot of myths about that . . . you get killed . . . you know, it depends on the person. If they think you ripped somebody off, you know, but if something happened, it happens. Then you don't have to pay. (28)

It was also important for the transporter to be up-front with the Colombian contact about the reason the load was lost. Sometimes a representative oversaw the transport and witnessed what happened, but in most cases there was not a witness, and the Colombian contact would come looking for the merchandise and the transportation team.

Payment for a lost load must be made to Colombian sources or through the broker in the United States, who would then send it to the broker or office to pay the insurance on the load. The cost varied depending on whether it was based on the price in Colombia, the price at the nearest body of land, or the retail price in the United States. The payment seems to depend on trust and on whether the Colombian sources perceived the loss as a business loss, meaning that law enforcement seized it, or as a theft. In the case of theft, the Colombian sources would expect to be compensated with the amount they would receive if the load was successful. Similarly if it was a robbery (for example, if Bahamian pirates stole the load and the transporter could not prove it), the Colombian sources would expect to be paid the cost of the cocaine in the Bahamas. Although the discussions and negotiations may be tenuous, the Colombian sources were reportedly interested in working it out because they did not want to lose a route.

Our sources reported that the Colombian sources expected one out of three loads to be lost as a function of the law enforcement threat, not human error. A loss by the transporters often was considered acceptable, and the operation appeared to rebound quickly. One smuggler described it the following way.

These people have thousands of kilos over there [Colombia]. You know, product is no problem. They want to get it to U.S. That's their main concern. So, I mean, if you lost a load, you know, hey, everything all right, did you lose equipment, who got arrested, take care of the person, make sure everything is going to be all right, and when are you going to do the next one? They are not worried about one hundred, one thousand, not even five thousand. They want to get—you know, they work by amounts, big amounts of cocaine. They want to make sure their product gets here. If they lose a load, they're going to keep trying not once, ten more times, until they get one in. It's a big profit. (1)

Brokers in the United States

Brokers in the United States work with the offices in Columbia to negotiate the sale price per kilo of the drugs coming over the border. They work for an independent broker or for the office in Colombia that was managing the transport into the United States. Brokers may also be asked to oversee the offload and to pick up and deliver the drugs. To perform these functions, the brokers were in communication with Colombian sources and the transportation team, but they actually worked for the Colombians. Brokers may also be in charge of delivering the money for the load and the profit back to Colombia or supplying the office in charge of money to move the money to Colombia, which may be done a multitude of different ways.

In many cases, the broker was responsible for working with the transportation team to pick up the load and for giving the load to the distribution group to sell or giving one part to the distributor and sold the rest to pay the transportation crew. In the first case, the broker would pick up the drugs, brings them to a distributor, and returns in a few days for his money.

The buyer in the U.S. only knows one guy, and that is the guy who does delivery, and he will deliver the merchandise, and the guy will give him the money. That's all. He doesn't know the offices. (13)

Because what I did was intermediate, if someone had something to sell, I would get someone to buy it and they would tell me a price, and I would ask for a different price from the people I knew. I had the buyers and I knew the ones who had it and the way they would bring it, if they brought to U.S., because they had it here. They would call me and tell me here is merchandise or I would go and ask for one or two kilos and they would say, "Okay, I'd get them for you." If they didn't have supply they would ask someone else if they had some or the other guy, until they got some. (9)

This office has people in here that they know, that they trust. It's just a matter of a phone call. I say, "I have this package for you. Would you take care of it?" And they say, "Okay, I'll take care of it." And then they have their own networking, which they have clients, calculate clients that are good for this amount of kilos per se or whatever. (13)

One of the brokers in the sample had a successful import-export business in Colombia that was a source of a legitimate income. This provided him with numerous contacts and knowledge of trade between Colombia and the United States. The access to or ownership of legitimate businesses enhanced the links between legitimate and illegitimate trade. A location such as South Florida, with substantial investment and involvement in international business, is perfect for drug smuggling.

I was an intermediary between the Colombians in Colombia and Miami—never touched or saw the drugs—just a businessman looking to facilitate. (15)

Retailers

Most of the smugglers in our sample were active from the early 1980s to the mid-1990s. At that time, the price of a kilo of cocaine in Colombia was $1,500 to $2,000, and prices in the United States fluctuated between $12,000 and $15,500, and as high as $20,000 for those selling in the northern sections of the United States. This made for considerable profit. However, one had to consider the cost of buying the paste in Peru and making it into powder, paying for protection, and paying transporters with sometimes as much as half the load. By the time the cocaine was sold on the street, someone may be making only $2,000 per kilo.

One smuggler discussed the profit that could be made with heroin. In 1989–1990, a unit (a kilogram) of heroin purchased in Asia for $5,260 could be sold on the street in the United States for $180,000 to $200,000. The transportation cost in this case would be minimal because one unit may be smuggled in by one "mule" on a commercial airline.

> We [Colombians] don't make the money. They make the money in American business. We pay them a lot of money. Out of one dollar, the Colombian guys get thirty-two cents. The other sixty-five cents are here in the United States.[3] Americans don't take any risk. They sell it for $15,000 per kilo and we make $2,000 to $2,500 per kilo and we have to pay the transportation to the United States and the warehouse about $6,000. (3)

Only if the cost per kilo got too low would the drugs not be shipped; one smuggler estimated that this threshold was about $10,000 per kilo.

Although we did not learn much about the payment received by a broker, one person in the sample described the additional profit he made by brokering to sell for a certain amount and then asking for a higher price and keeping the profit.

Returning Profits to Colombia

Most of the smugglers could not speak to the methods used to move the money back to Colombia, except to say that there was always a Colombian connection in the United States to move the money or that the organization was small enough for the transportation crew members to do it themselves. Four of the smugglers who worked for Colombians had been involved in money laundering, however, and they were able to discuss the methods they used to hide the proceeds they made transporting drugs into the United States.

One of the launderers owned a car dealership in Miami and would accept more than the cash value of a car and clean the rest of the money by laundering it through businesses in Panama. He also oversaw an operation to move large amounts of money from Miami to Argentina and then to Uruguay. The money would be shipped to Argentina in suitcases; the organization would pay officials in Argentina (15 percent of the funds) to offload the suitcases; and then the money would be deposited in banks in Uruguay. The second, less sophisticated smuggler would move money into eight to ten different accounts in the United States and move money through front operations in Colombia and Miami. He would send a fax to Colombia to verify each deposit. In this case, ten people ran the money office, eight in Colombia and two in Miami. A third smuggler, who knew of the methods used by the money office, talked about hiding the money in heavy equipment and sending it back to Colombia, or sending it in cashier's checks and using front corporations. A fourth got involved in smuggling drugs because an organization had begun using his warehouse and asked him to write checks.

Summary

Our sample of high-level drug smugglers was able to confirm information about how drug smuggling operations have evolved since the demise of cartels in the 1990s. The smugglers confirmed the shift away from large centralized groups to smaller groups working together to organize loads and transport drugs into the United States. They were able to describe each of these groups and indicate how they functioned together to move the drugs. Because most of the smugglers had direct experience with the actual transportation of drugs to the United States, we received the most detail about this aspect of the operation.

The smugglers described various groups working both in Colombia and the United States to organize loads of drugs, transport those drugs to the United States, and return profits to Colombia. Core groups or offices organized specific aspects of the operation (generating the load, transporting it, and distributing it), while multiple specialized groups or individuals supported these efforts (working independently or for specific offices). The result was that no single person controlled multiple aspects of the operation; instead, a series of people organized specific aspects.

In its purest sense, the current structure could perform much more efficiently than was possible under the more centralized cartels. Presumably, competition among groups (farmers, transporters, sellers, etc.) would keep operational costs down and profits high, enabling people with responsibility for particular aspects of the operation to take advantage of the increased options and easily shift or vary approaches (e.g., routes, methods, and money transfers) to avoid suspicion and detection by authorities. While we were not able to confirm this outcome with our group of smugglers or discuss other changes in business practices in Colombia, we could see how the current structure has evolved to overcome weaknesses associated with the structure of the 1970s and 1980s.

Most noteworthy about what was learned from the smugglers is that smuggling operations of the 1990s may have had more members than earlier thought and may have been better protected because of the larger number of small, isolated cells. As one smuggler described the process:

It is like a parent company shipping to a subsidiary. (24)

This is especially important for law enforcement because tactics relied on in the past may no longer work as effectively. For example, law enforcement efforts to infiltrate smuggling organizations are less likely to have a significant impact, given the decentralization of power and knowledge and the sheer number of networks now working to transport drugs into the United States.

Additionally, drugs and money are no longer linked; there are two different networks controlling the movement of drugs into the United States and money back into Colombia. Although breaking large entities into small groups may reduce the size of the loads an organization is responsible for, an increase in the number of people moving drugs out of the country—and money back in—will make it more difficult for law enforcement strategies to have an impact on drug shipments.

> Worse for law enforcement. Too many people now. I would say 90 percent of Colombia smuggles drugs, and [the] other 10 percent, it might not be you or other guy, but his cousin or nephew is involved with drugs. So their money, whatever funds they are getting, it's diverted from drugs, you know. (22)

> They [the groups in Cali] help each other. If we talk about a cartel, we can talk about the Orjuelas, Miguel, and Gilberto that are in prison. They are the chiefs, the powerful, but . . . there are smaller groups and also thousands of little groups that all help each other, ask each other for merchandise. Right now, that [cartels] is destroyed. Right now, there are about forty or fifty people working, so this is an endless war. (2)

The other difficulty is that the core of the networks is still linked by culture and secrecy and the impact of breaking any one of the cells is minimized by the difficulty of spreading the impact to other cells. For example, the manager of transport does not know the manager of distribution. Therefore, if the distributor was caught, law enforcement would have to go through the distributor to the broker in the United States and may get to the manager of transport or the broker in Colombia, but law enforcement was unlikely to get to the heads of each of the offices. In response to a question about interdiction strategy and tactics of catching the guy on the bottom and flipping him to get to the next guy and the next guy until they get Mr. Big, one suspect told us that

> Mr. Big go home and little kid stay here because you only know a little bit. It's the big guy who is the one to go home [Colombia]. (32)

This feeling of immunity from law enforcement was reinforced by the smugglers' perception of the least risky position in a smuggling operation; many felt that the best role was the owner in Colombia because he was safe from interdiction efforts targeted at shipments of drugs.

As the next two chapters describe, this decentralization is coupled with multiple options for moving drugs into the United States and various players, the most vulnerable of whom know the least about the smuggling event.

4 Movement of Drugs

ndividuals were asked to describe, based on their experience, typical drug smuggling events from source country to the United States. These descriptions and information about the offenses for which the smugglers were convicted provide specifics of the ways drugs are transported into the United States, as well as of the ways smugglers avoid being detected. The information presented in this chapter sheds light on the dynamic nature of drug smuggling events, the risks associated with different transportation methods, and strategies used to minimize those risks.

Transportation Routes

Source to Midpoint

Colombians are in charge of transporting loads of drugs out of Colombia. Most often, the drugs are moved from Colombia to a mid-shipment location using a transporter hired and overseen by Colombians. The method of transport described by smugglers most often was by airplane, with the load either dropped or landed in such countries as the Bahamas, Cuba, Aruba, Haiti, Honduras, and Puerto Rico. A number of smugglers identified a landing strip on the Guajira Peninsula controlled by drug traffickers and often used by planes departing with drugs.

In other cases, the drugs are moved directly to the United States or Puerto Rico from Colombia. In those cases, the transport out of Colombia is set up by an organizer of transport in either Colombia or the United States, depending on the method of shipment. Typically, a commercial vessel or large fishing boat transports the load. A freighter was used to transport drugs to Philadelphia in one case and to Puerto Rico in another.

In one case, drugs were moved from Colombia to Venezuela to be loaded on a commercial vessel bound for Puerto Rico. Crossing the border between the two countries was described as very easy, with the eight thousand kilos hidden in a compartment in the gas tank of a commercial vehicle. Moving the drugs this short distance prevented the shipment departure country from being Colombia, reducing suspicion a little. Another smuggler described a typical route from Barranquilla to Santa Marta by plane, which then landed in San Andreas. San Andreas is a vacation spot for many Colombians, and the smuggler described a connection with U.S. law enforcement agents that allowed the landing and movement of the load to boats for transport to Isle del Maiz off the Yucatan Peninsula for transport to the Florida Keys on shrimp boats.

Regardless of method, the organizer of the transport out of Colombia and the organizer of the transport into the United States communicate with one another. Because the smugglers we spoke with were primarily responsible for transport into the United States, the logistics involved in moving a load out of Colombia were unknown to most members of our sample. However, the nature of communication between the two organizers was known. The organizer of the transport in Colombia is in charge of identifying when the load can move and its method, as well as of identifying longitude and latitude points for the pickup. The Colombian organizer is also responsible for the mid-shipment point and is, therefore, responsible for paying off officials or airport crews and hiring the crew necessary to ensure safe transfer.

Midpoint to the United States

Most of the smugglers we talked to were not responsible for organizing the effort in the mid-shipment country, though they did say that the manager of the transport could negotiate the route with the organizer in Colombia and raise his country-specific concerns. Most of the transporters we spoke with were responsible for organizing specifics of transport from mid-shipment to the point of offload.

The Bahamas have been a favorite mid-shipment point for transport of both marijuana and cocaine for many years. Fifteen of the smugglers reported either having personally organized transports from the Bahamas to the United States or having experience with the actual transportation. The Bahamas are made up of more than seven hundred islands, half of which are uninhabited. It is as difficult for Bahamian officials to patrol these islands as it is for U.S. law enforcement to follow a smuggler through the islands during a chase. The islands are only forty miles from Miami, which makes travel in all types of boats feasible. The multiple islands also present an opportunity to bury the drugs if law enforcement presence is detected. Corruption on the island allows for the purchase of flight plans and for landing planes from Colombia, making the transfer of loads more secure.

There is one downside to the Bahamas: the presence of pirates. This forces smugglers to move quickly if they use the area as a mid-shipment zone. One smuggler described the situation in the following manner.

> [T]he whole island [the Bahamas] is a jungle and surrounded by pirates. They go around in these big boats, and if they find drugs, they will kill you and take the drugs and sell them to other Americans that come over. Yeah, there is no law out

there. Your enemies are the pirates and whoever you come across out there. (24)

This fear led some smugglers to switch to alternate routes or to begin carrying weapons during the transport.

Cuba was used by at least four of the smugglers. They preferred Cuba primarily because they believed it was the most secure mid-shipment point, since the government could be paid off and U.S. law enforcement could not enter the flight zone around it. Cuba is also a short distance from Miami. First the plane would fly over Cuba to let officials know it was there, and then the smugglers would airdrop the load off the coast of Cuba for boats that would bring it to Florida.

Other mid-shipment points that were mentioned were Puerto Rico, Mexico, Haiti, Jamaica, Honduras, and the Dominican Republic. Each of these areas is used by transporters to exchange the load being flown from Colombia by landing or by airdropping the load to boats waiting to transport the drugs to the United States. The drugs that come through Puerto Rico may also be brought into the United States by plane, and drugs from Mexico are often driven across the border. Two smugglers mentioned paying off Mexican authorities to facilitate the smuggling. Mexico is considered by many of the smugglers to be an easy route because of the possibilities for corruption and payoffs for information. However, like the Bahamas, there is also an internal threat from guerillas.

The United States

The end point of the transportation responsibility varied among smugglers. Some were in charge of transport, offloading, and delivery; some were in charge of offloading and delivery only; and others were involved in just the transport. In almost all cases, the drugs were brought into Florida, most often the Florida Keys, Miami, and Fort Lauderdale. The only exceptions were drugs moved through Puerto Rico or Mexico and via commercial vessels and planes with the final destination of the West or East Coast.

Many transporters tried to stay away from offloading and distribution because they did not want to be connected to the drugs while on land. In these cases, a phone call would be made from the transporter to the manager, or the manager or someone working for the manager would meet the transporter and take over the load. Many of the transportation managers saw touching the drugs as a lower-class role, not part of the "businessman's" role, and felt that offloading and distribution presented unnecessary risks. Someone working for the manager would meet the transportation team to inform the team that the load was in. The manager would then contact Colombia to report that the load was ready for pickup. At that point, the transportation manager would coordinate with the broker in the United States to drop off the load. The smugglers claimed a relationship with the person in Colombia but not with the broker in the United States.

> I never bring that [load] in, I remain clean all the time. I don't want to get busted. I furnish them the automobile, and they put it in a parking lot of a shopping center. I have somebody drive it to a warehouse. I take my share and sell it. (33)

> My involvement in drugs at that moment, I've never seen the merchandise. You know, the merchandise, I only organized it, and somebody goes to West Palm Beach to pick up five hundred kilos, and somebody goes over there. I don't want to go to this house to look at merchandise, something like that. (3)

When a private boat transported the load into Florida, the load was either brought to a house on the water, where the drugs would be offloaded and delivered, or to a marina, where the boat would either sit until nightfall or be transported to a warehouse.

> We had a house in North Miami, and the boat would come behind the house, park the boat behind the house, and let it sit there for a couple of hours. Then we'd unload the drugs

into the house, and we would have cars, you know, inside the garage, put them in the cars and take them to the Colombians. (22)

The boat was usually moved to a warehouse when the load was hidden in a compartment, so that the boat could be taken out of the water and cut to remove the load. In one case, the smuggler brought a decoy boat to replace the boat he was removing and bringing to the warehouse. The captain of the boat or the person who built the compartment usually removed the drugs from the compartment. Once removed, the load would be picked up or delivered by someone on the transport team or someone in the distribution group.

I'll come in [to the warehouse] with a couple guys, and I'll take the boat apart. I'll count what it is I'm going to give the Colombians, and I'll count whatever I am going to keep in another car, give the car to the Colombians and take the other car to wherever I am going to keep that deposit at until they pay me all of my money. (22)

The drugs seemed to be exchanged at one of three places: a private residence, a warehouse, or a parking lot in a shopping center. A parking lot seemed to be favored when more than one group was picking up a load. Shopping centers were viewed favorably because they do not draw suspicion when a car or van is left to be picked up by someone else. Shopping center parking lots are also open. Exchanging the load in a public place made the operation quick and less personal and allowed the use of techniques to check for surveillance and the presence of law enforcement. Waiting for a pickup at a house or warehouse was more personal and involved more stress and potential delays.

Offloaded in Keys. Put in different sources of transportation. Sometimes we use cars, vans, Winnebagos, whatever we thought was more convenient and less suspicious. We'd put it [merchandise] in those vehicles and just, you know, put a couple of old people in it and say I'm going to give you fifty grand. Just drive it to this place and leave it there and you leave, you know? (1)

One smuggler (16) talked about the method he used to drop off the load. On arrival of the load, he would call or fax Colombia with the arrangements for pickup, indicating that the car was in good working order and that the driver was clean-cut and had a driver's license. Once he and another person arrived at the specified location, they would pick up the driver and drive him around in one car, while the other person would pick up the car and drive it to the warehouse. Both would check for the presence of law enforcement. The car would be checked for tracking devices, loaded with drugs, and brought to a different location. Then the driver would be brought back and would leave with the load. The transporter would follow the driver to his next destination.

In two cases, smugglers mentioned the presence of a representative of the Colombian organization during the transport or the offloading and delivery of the merchandise. This seemed to occur when the transporter or route was new and the Colombians did not feel their usual trust.

Points of Entry

The smugglers were asked to identify the easiest and most difficult points of entry into the United States. Although most smugglers said that the toughest part of the transport was bringing the load into the United States, they had different opinions about the easiest point of entry. Six of the nineteen smugglers mentioned that active smugglers consider Mexico to be the easiest route because of the three thousand miles of border to be patrolled and because poverty offers significant opportunities for bribery and corruption. Five stated that ports of entry on the water are easy, especially in Florida. On the other hand, two said Miami was difficult because of DEA activities in the Bahamas and because

Miami has law enforcement intelligence networks. Two others mentioned that any ports where they have contacts are easy. When asked what ports of entry they found most difficult, five of the smugglers mentioned airports and commercial ports because of the increased law enforcement presence. Only one responded that there were no hard points of entry.

Methods of Transport

Based on smugglers' direct experiences, we collected details on the different methods used to transport drugs, the risks specific to those methods, and the strategies used to minimize risks. Since most of the smugglers transported drugs into Florida, it is not surprising that we were able to collect the most detail on transporting drugs via private vessels, but the smugglers were also able to describe other methods.

Private Vessels

The chances of flying a plane from Colombia or a place north of Colombia directly into the United States without detection are slim. Therefore, most smuggling of drugs into the United States uses a boat of some type. Eighteen of the smugglers shared their direct experiences with this method of bringing in drugs.

In most cases, the drugs were flown to a mid-shipment point like Cuba, the Bahamas, Honduras, or a body of water and either landed or airdropped to fast boats, fishing boats, or yachts. A few smugglers mentioned that, when possible, they preferred to land the plane because of the potential for loss when loads are dropped. Airdropping also made the determination of culpability more difficult when loads were lost and the drugs were not all accounted for, especially if the drugs were not directly handed off to someone after the drop.

In the 1980s, the drugs were transported from the Bahamas or Cuba in "go-fast" boats—usually modified cigarette boats with two or three engines that held approximately four hundred kilos.

Because of the popularity of go-fast boats among smugglers, law enforcement became suspicious of anyone using this type of boat, and go-fast boats began to fall out of favor. At about the same time, smugglers were also using lobster or shrimp boats to move drugs, especially marijuana, into the United States. These boats offered three things go-fast boats did not: anonymity, the option of building a compartment to hide the drugs, and the ability to hold loads larger than four hundred kilos.

As cocaine became a more popular drug to transport, compartments within boats and the use of less obvious boats continued to be favored. Yachts and sailboats that were able to make longer trips made it possible to hide loads in compartments and allowed for new routes to be traversed. These more expensive boats were also a product of more sophisticated methods. More sophisticated compartments could be built on them, and smugglers felt that law enforcement would be less reluctant to tear apart an expensive boat on a hunch.

Small crews were used to transport loads via speedboats or fishing boats. Two to three people could handle a load, which was usually less than five hundred kilos per boat. Small crews limited the number of codefendants and reduced the possibility of snitches. Some of the smugglers preferred to use Americans or Cubans to bring in loads because they blended in with other boaters. In bigger operations, there were others involved besides the boat crew, such as the manager of the transport, people on the ground to provide security, someone to drive the bait boat, people to watch law enforcement stations, and people to oversee transfer of the load.

Both airdrops and transfers via boat were usually done at night. When traveling by speedboat, the loads were brought in at night to the Florida Keys or to a house in South Florida. The night drop was better because law enforcement was suspicious of speedboats, and there was less intense law enforcement on the water at night. One smuggler used three boats to bring in the load: one with the load, one to provide support if the loaded boat broke down, and a third with no drugs on board that acted as a decoy. Other smugglers traveled in pairs so that one could provide support if the boat with the load had mechanical problems, making it unnecessary for the loaded boat to call the Coast Guard for assistance.

When fishing or lobster boats were used, the load was usually brought in and out of the marina with the daily fishing traffic. Captains of these boats would also go to great lengths to use props to indicate that they had been on the water fishing all day (e.g., bait, food, beer, lobsters, fish, and fishing equipment). A popular strategy was to smuggle during fishing tournaments or regattas, registering a decoy and switching boats as the race concluded. One smuggler mentioned that he came into the marina at noon, when the Coast Guard and sheriff's department took their lunch break.

Boat captains and transportation managers of all types of boats used a number of tactics to avoid detection, including blending in with normal traffic by arriving and departing with other similar boats, having good navigational equipment, using commercial routes, remaining close to land and other islands, and being on the water during holidays, regattas, and weekends. One smuggler noted that he spent a lot of money on boats and fishing equipment because U.S. Customs agents were less suspicious of boats and gear that looked legitimate. To avoid generating law enforcement suspicion of an individual boat, the owners changed the name and registration, painted the boat, and sometimes switched the registration to the country that was going to be the mid-shipment point.

> Go out and buy old boat and I registered that in my old
> name. Then I took the numbers off of it and put it on my
> boat. So, therefore—and then I also painted my boat, changed
> the color of my boat and also changed the appearance. (12)

Smugglers avoided a number of actions that they felt were too suspicious, such as having people on the boat whose ethnicities were unlike those of other boaters (that is, captains preferred to use Americans or Cubans, who blended in), traveling during bad weather, carrying extra fuel, not having fish on a fishing boat, and being on the water during odd hours.

> [The] hardest part of smuggling is time that you have on the vessel or on the vehicle transporting, especially if it's—if it's a large quantity, the transport part is real slow. (4)

> The person that mostly has a chance of getting caught is the person on the boat. Because they are really heavily guarded. You have all sorts of new things out there with the balloon things. The other AWAC things. There's so many different ways that you can get caught, plus the ones we don't even know that they keep secret, that its really hard to get in unless it's very short trips, you know, maybe three or four hours at the most. (4)

The smugglers employed a variety of strategies to track law enforcement and assess the risk of being caught. A number mentioned having someone monitor the boats arriving at and departing from the marine patrol or Customs and Coast Guard stations. They mentioned trying to document the schedules and patterns of patrol as well as trying to identify the location of patrol boats that had left dock. One smuggler and his group went on non-smuggling boat rides to survey interdiction efforts and identify the locations of law enforcement boats. Smugglers also used scanners and identified law enforcement channels on high-frequency radios to monitor enforcement activities. They used lookouts on bridges and highways to note law enforcement movement. Three smugglers mentioned trying to gain intelligence through their contacts in the military and trying to bribe U.S. Customs Service and U.S. Coast Guard officials to share information on interdiction activities. Some smugglers used planes or other boats to identify whether law enforcement was tracking boats in the water. Two used transponders to see whether tracking devices had been put on their boats. Another identified spots where sweep radios or scanning devices crossed and altered his route to come in through the overlapped areas.

Despite these precautions, many of the smugglers did not worry about tracking law enforcement when they were on the water because they could do nothing about it, and methods to detect tails can be more suspicious than preventive. Boat captains usually used GPS, forty-eight-mile radar, and thirty-two-mile radar to identify whether law enforcement was tracking them, which gave them enough time to identify whether law enforcement was suspicious. If they were being followed, they had a few options: they could surrender, throw the load overboard, sink the boat, return to the mid-shipment point, or try to outrun their pursuers. If the load was not in a compartment, throwing the load overboard was not a good option because the load was often packaged to float, so it took time to sink, and there was no way to be absolutely sure the pursuer was law enforcement until the boat that was following was right next to the smuggler's boat. If the drugs were not in a compartment and the boat was fast, smugglers generally returned to the mid-shipment point, often Cuba or the Bahamas. If the boat was unlikely to outrun law enforcement, the only option was to allow law enforcement to board the boat and try to find the drugs. From what the smugglers told us, this is not a bad option; the smugglers in the sample claimed that law enforcement boarded and released almost every boat in which the load was hidden in a compartment.

If the methods employed by the transportation manager to detect law enforcement identified suspicious activity, he would communicate with the crew members and tell them to wait it out if they could, to change course, or to stop in the water and throw out their fishing lines. Communication could usually be established between the manager and the crew via radio or cellular phone. In some cases, usually when using independent transporters, the captain and the person bringing in the load to the transfer point cannot communicate, and the captain may have to wait or return without the load. Some of the managers mentioned visiting the planned rendezvous point ahead of time, calling other transporters to ask about activity, or calling a contact in the area and asking, "How is the fishing?" If there were "sharks" in the water, the manager would get the coordinates of the informant's location and hold off for a day or so.

> It's like being in the water with a shark. Sharks are very sensitive to your state of mind. Fear is not an option. (12)

None of the boat smugglers mentioned resorting to violence when faced with law enforcement, not even when the Bahamas adopted a shoot policy.

> [There was risk because] they were seizing a lot at the time. Interdiction seemed to be working better or something. That would have trouble over the Bahamas from the authorities, which I'm sure they were paying off. . . . hear stuff from other people, but generally the Cuban guy [his contact to Colombia] would come to me and say, "Hey they got problems over in the Bahamas," or "We're going to call it off a week." (5)

Shift in Methods

A monumental change in the patterns of those who used boats was in the use of compartments. Compartments were first used with marijuana and were not sophisticated because they had to be the size of a room to store the amount that was being smuggled at the time. As law enforcement pressure increased in the 1980s, marijuana became less popular; cocaine became the drug of choice; and the technique of using compartments remained in favor. However, the compartments built to hold cocaine were much more sophisticated. They were more likely to be built between the hull and the floor, usually near the gas tank, because drug dogs cannot detect anything mixed with oil.

Fifteen of the smugglers mentioned the use of compartments. One smuggler talked about the seal on the compartment that made it difficult for drug dogs to find the load.

> So the only way to avoid this was to make a seal—tight—sealed compartments. So what I used to do, I used to build the compartment, put fiberglass inside of it, paint it with gel coat, and then on the trap door, I would set it up with rubber all around it, and I would set up a vacuum pack. (16)

This same smuggler indicated that his boat had been boarded twice and that a dog never sniffed out the drugs. A naval architect measured his boat when it was caught and could not find the drugs. Another smuggler who used compartments claimed that he had been stopped about ten times by the U.S. Coast Guard, but the officers never found the drugs. One of his techniques was to build a number of hatches to make the search more convenient and less likely to be too intrusive.

Another individual had considerable experience in engineering boats and working with fiberglass. During the early 1980s, he worked for a cigarette boat company, making boats from scratch, and he had risen to master craftsman status while learning a variety of sophisticated techniques for reengineering boats. In addition, he had a number of contacts in the boat-building industry, and he continued to count on them during his smuggling days. He described the way he added a false bottom to a boat and put in a second hidden compartment in considerable detail.

> It's sealed off [the tank]. I used the same material that they used on the boat to make the boat fiberglass. It was sealed completely so there wouldn't be no smell. In fact, we had a couple of loads where they got stopped by U.S. Customs and they took the boat down to Miami and they tore up the boat and they never found anything. In 1994 when I was arrested, when I finally gave the boat to the U.S. Customs lady and she found out that the boat had drugs, she called the

agent that was working on that search and he couldn't believe it. The only thing that I altered was the fuel capacity
and the water capacity. I used to work [smuggle] in the day-
time. I used to come in on Saturdays at three in the after-
noon right through the cut in front of Customs, in front of
the Coast Guard. Why? Because they never suspected that
that boat would do that, but if you running out there at
night, you've got a bigger chance of being caught. (22)

I would have it set up where I would have the trailer and a
ramp all ready and the process of that is different from completely from what maybe some of you had heard. I'll bring
the truck and put the trailer—we would bring the truck with
a boat and a trailer. That way if somebody is on the ramp,
nobody is going to suspect because if you see a truck and a
trailer coming into a ramp somebody is going to pick up. If
anybody is looking at this situation, they're thinking the guy
is going fishing. Three or four hours later here comes another boat just like it but you forgot already about it because
there's thirty boats already gone through there and now the
truck comes back in, in the water, picks up the right [drug-
laden] boat, and takes off. (22)

One smuggler described the process to conceal cocaine as
follows. The load was packed under the gas tank, and the cover
was sealed with a sealing compound. Then the tank was dropped
in, and two-part foam with black food coloring was used to seal
in the tank. To get the load out, the foam would have to be cut
out, the gas pumped out of the tank, the sealing compound cut
through, and the tank pulled out to access the drugs. Before leaving the pickup point, the smuggler would fill the gas tank so that
law enforcement would be less likely to want to empty the tank to
check the possibility of a compartment in the boat. This same
smuggler mentioned that he was very confident about his compartment, although he did bring methylethylketone (MEK) in

case the drug dog began sniffing it out. He described the compartment in his single-engine cabin cruiser as follows.

> I also loaded a thousand pounds of concrete block in the boat and drew the water line and I painted the water line with a thousand pounds of concrete block in the boat. That way the boat was loaded with cocaine, it looked absolutely normal. And there would be fish in the coolers and there would be beer in the coolers and there would be bait slopped over the deck and just generally looked like fishing. If they ever wanted to check underneath the floor [of the gas tank] they were going to have to pump 110 gallons of gas overboard. They were going to have to violate some of their own [environmental] laws. The best time to smuggle would be the Fourth of July weekend, Labor Day weekend, Memorial Day weekend, weekends with enormous amounts of boat traffic. I had a tube of MEK (methylethylketone) an extremely volatile solvent and if a dog gets a good nose full of it, it does something to his olfactory sensories center. (12)

Another smuggler had a compartment with a hydraulic system built into his fishing boat, by far the most sophisticated compartment described by any of the smugglers.

In general, most of the smugglers transporting loads in the 1990s were using boats with some sort of compartment, and most felt that there was little chance of detection with this technique, as it is difficult to do a comprehensive search of a boat on the water. This is why smugglers build additional hatches and create options so that law enforcement agents who board their boats feel like they have conducted good searches. Some smugglers felt that, in general, law enforcement was lazy and did not look that hard.

Many smugglers openly acknowledged that it would be virtually impossible to identify a compartment unless you compared a boat similar to the smuggler's boat. This could be done only on shore or as part of a seizure. Others found that the only way law enforcement ever found drugs was to break up the boat.

> They found it. I mean if you put the boat through a grinder, you're going to find it sooner or later. So that's how they found the secret compartment. (22)

> [Law enforcement] wouldn't find the compartment because [it] did not fit profile; there was not any . . . suspicious situation, and my demeanor was that of being very relaxed. (12)

Compartments protected smugglers from law enforcement and offered more security from theft and robbery for the organizers and owners of the load. One outcome of the shift to compartments involved the offloading procedures, with smugglers no longer needed on the marinas or public ramps because the boats had to be out of the water to be taken apart for load removal. This was often done at a warehouse. It also removed the option for passing the load off to smaller boats because this could not be done in the water.

Commercial Vessels

Although Haitian freighters have been moving loads of drugs up the Miami River for many years, not until the 1990s did containers become a popular way to bring cocaine into the United States. Five of the smugglers cited commercial freighters as the easiest way to bring drugs into the United States. Some considered it the safest way to increase the size of the load, often up to five thousand kilos. Others saw it as yet another situation in which volume overwhelms enforcement capacity; eight hundred vessels arrive in the Port of Miami every day, with thousands of containers to be searched.

> They're [Customs] not that good. Not that smart, and even if they were, it's impossible to cover—they've been told. So

we're right back to where, without an informant, no one gets caught. (24)

Ten of the smugglers in our sample were involved, in one way or another, with a load of drugs brought in by freighter. Unfortunately, the specifics of these operations were unknown to them in many cases. One option when using a freighter is to hide the load among the legal products or in the walls of the container. Another option is to bring the load all the way into the port or to offload while in the water.

The earlier commercial vessel loads took the latter approach and offloaded to smaller boats that brought the drugs to shore. Before he was caught, one smuggler was planning to offload three thousand to five thousand kilos from a freighter to three or four yachts waiting off the coast of Florida. One used commercial freighters to smuggle cocaine from Aruba to Holland. In another case, cocaine was hidden in cylinders on the bottom of a commercial vessel, a banana boat. Another smuggler described using boats shipping suntan oil to move marijuana loads into the United States.

Only recently did smuggling operations become sophisticated enough to set up offloading operations at the port. Offloading drugs from containers and delivering them to a buyer is a complex operation. First, the drugs must be hidden. In three cases, they were hidden among the merchandise and identified by different markings or their location on the pallet. In one operation, the load was hidden in boxes of laundry detergent being shipped from Venezuela to Puerto Rico. In another case, the load was hidden in pallets of clay pots imported into Miami via Colombia.

Another vessel contained three thousand kilos of cocaine in the false wall of a container bringing cement to Cuba. When the vessel was off the Florida coast, the crew began drilling out the wall of the container and threw the load overboard, attached by rope. The load was then picked up by speedboats and brought into Florida. The vessel continued to slowly move toward Cuba for the whole time the operation was going on. In another interesting operation, a boat with a hidden compartment that was going to

Panama was loaded with drugs and then transported on a commercial freighter until it met up with its decoy. The boats were switched at night, and the boat loaded with drugs was brought into the United States.

Using commercial vessels to bring in loads requires larger crews because larger loads are needed to make a profit. There is also the need for more coordination when bringing in a load via commercial vessel and organizing the transfer in the water or at the port. These factors make commercial vessels an expensive option.

> It seems like there is a lot of expense for these ships, they have to pay four or five people in Colombia, so they have to have big quantities in order to make a profit. (2)

Private Planes

Before the U.S. government began using Airborne Warning and Control Systems (AWACS), planes were used to bring the loads all the way into U.S. territory and for drops in the Gulf and Caribbean waters. When U.S. law enforcement started using AWACS and balloons, the smuggling operation changed dramatically. Planes continued to transport loads of drugs, but to mid-shipment points—usually Mexico, Panama, the Bahamas, Cuba, and islands closer to Colombia—rather than directly into the United States. The loads were then picked up by boats, the sizes varying with the distance, and brought to the United States. This change in method, which was consistent across many of the smuggling operations discussed by the twelve smugglers who had experience using planes to move the loads, illustrates the dynamic nature of drug smuggling and reactions to changes in enforcement tactics. The general impression among smugglers is that flying a plane to the United States is dangerous because it can be detected easily.

> Planes are history, because there is more surveillance now. (71)

At about the same time, the smugglers reported, Americans became less likely to be piloting the planes. Pilots flying loads of marijuana in the 1970s were described as "old vets" with past military flying experience. When Americans were flying loads, the planes would usually be kept in the United States and flown from there to Colombia and back. One smuggler claimed that he kept his plane in the United States because of thieves in other countries.

> The pilots were gringos. Especially, I used to like them because they were mostly all vets. I mean Vietnam and Korea and all this. War is—the United States was involved in. It drove those people crazy, and they loved the excitement. (29)

Pilots flying loads of cocaine in the 1980s and 1990s were usually identified as Colombian, or their citizenship was unknown because hiring the pilot was the Colombian representative's responsibility.

When flown, a load of usually between five hundred and eight hundred kilos left Colombia on a Piper Navajo, Compass 2, DC-3, or DC-6 (basically, hollowed-out small passenger planes). The plane either landed or airdropped the load to transporters waiting to take the load into the United States. A few of the smugglers mentioned pilots departing from Colombia using a five-mile-long landing strip on the Guajira Peninsula. The planes usually flew in at night to avoid suspicion and flew low to prevent detection by radar.

Often, a legitimate flight plan would be obtained so that the plane looked less suspicious when monitored by AWACS. The flight plans that were purchased were not the exact flight patterns, so there was still some element of risk as the pilot tried to reach the flight route or diverted from it to land or drop the load. Someone would also watch from the ground when the plane was flying in to determine whether the pilot was being followed; if so, the pilot would return to Colombia. Similarly, if a pilot flying from the United States to Colombia to get a load was being followed, he would try to make it past Cuba because U.S. law enforcement was unlikely to continue farther south.

When planning the transport of a load by plane, an important consideration was whether the plane could land, which usually meant paying off someone working at the airport or in a mid-shipment location. This was especially the case in Mexico and the Bahamas. Paying off airport staff in Mexico and the Bahamas was not described as a simple task, and it may or may not have been part of the smugglers' area of responsibility. Many smugglers preferred landing the load, because doing so left less room for error and lost loads. If the load was landed, a count could occur at the transfer point. Landing the load also limited the size of the flight crew, since a crew member did not need to assist in dumping the load. On the other hand, landing the load required hiring offloaders and possibly securing a safe house to store the load until transport continued.

If a landing strip was not available, the next question was where the load would be dropped. Dropping the load also involved protection, which typically involved a few smugglers from Cuba. More recently, orchestrating security from Cuba was the responsibility of the Colombian end of the transport. The load could also be dropped off in Puerto Rico or in the Gulf or Caribbean.

If the load was going to be dropped at night, it would need to be packaged. The packaging would need to be durable enough to withstand a drop into the ocean and a pickup by boat. The pilot would be given latitude and longitude points, would circle around the location, and would have a copilot throw the load or would use rollers inside the plane to drop bales out the door. Some smugglers talked about identifying multiple drop points in case law enforcement presence prohibited the use of the original drop point.

> [E]verybody knew where law enforcement radar was located. People on the inside—you know where the Coast Guard is that particular day. (33)

In another case, the smuggler talked about meeting the load with two types of boats: a yacht with a compartment and a speedboat. Depending on the circumstances, a decision between "speed or stash" could be made.

Two smugglers talked about the impact of AWACS on their organization. One mentioned that routes and methods had been altered to avoid bringing the plane north of Cuba. Another mentioned the detection and response by pilots.

> One fellow would fly his airplane to here [Cuba], and if he saw the thing [AWACS], he would divert and go another way, and if it wasn't there—and I guess he didn't—they had some way of knowing if the thing was there or not, and it seems to me it was positioned so they would cover air traffic through this area here [between Cuba and the tip of Florida]. (24)

Commercial Planes

Only six of the smugglers in the sample had experience in smuggling drugs using commercial airlines or cargo planes. This may be because many smugglers consider moving drugs through airports to be considerably more risky than moving drugs through boats or vehicles. Smuggling drugs using mules or hidden in suitcases is seen as less profitable because only small loads can be transported and the chance of losing a load is significant, given the law enforcement presence at U.S. airports. Three smugglers in the sample specifically called this method the most difficult.[1] One stated that

> You have to be a complete idiot to try to bring drugs into the country on your body. They search you in Customs. (24)

> I think that if you tried to bring some drugs into the United States and you put them on your body going into the airport with all the dogs and all the Customs agents they got

around, I think I will say the airport will be one of the hardest places. (7)

Based on the cases cited, between five and twenty kilos may be transported in suitcases and one and a half to three kilos on or in the body of a mule. In two of the three cases in which the drugs were hidden inside suitcases, airline baggage handlers were bribed to divert the luggage from international to domestic flights. One case involved baggage handlers in St. Martin and the other at a New York airport. The individuals involved in the second case also used someone working at Miami International to meet the mules coming off the flight and escort them past Customs. The baggage handlers in St. Martin were paid $2,000 a kilo, making $400,000 a day for no more than four hours' work.

In the third case, the suitcases were loaded with regular luggage from Colombia and brought through Customs at Miami International Airport. In two additional but separate cases, the drugs were hidden in liquid and brought through Customs. The load hidden in Haitian oil went undetected, and another, in duty-free bottles, was detected.

The smugglers developed a number of tactics to prevent U.S. Customs from detecting the load. For example, one group of smugglers put grease, mustard, and pepper in suitcases so the dogs would not smell the drugs and added carbon paper to blacken the picture as the suitcase was sent through X-ray. Another group used a mixture of toothpaste and what was described as Haitian dog repellent to repel the dogs.

One group used American couples with U.S. passports to bring loads back from a pseudo vacation in Colombia. The travelers were also told that if they saw the suitcases lined up against the wall, they should keep walking and not pick them up. The organizers would also make sure that their flights were arriving during busy hours.[2]

In another case, heroin was transported on a cargo plan from Asia to Puerto Rico and hidden in legal merchandise. And in another operation, drugs were flown to New York and Miami from Puerto Rico using an express package service.

> We have people work [at an overnight shipping company] certain times of the week. They would ship it, and they would deliver it in the city that we wanted. (73)

Vehicles

Only two smugglers identified experience using land vehicles to move drugs into the United States. One moved drugs from Colombia to Venezuela in a compartment in the gas tank of a commercial truck. The other used his warehouse in California to store cocaine after driving the drugs across the Mexican border. Trucks would either travel all the way from Colombia or had picked up a load that had been brought by plane from Colombia. In a scenario presented by one smuggler, a plane brought one hundred thousand kilos of cocaine to Mexico. The landing strip had been reserved through bribes of Mexican officials, and loads of about seven hundred kilos were brought over the border during a thirty-day period. The load was broken up for practicality and to minimize loss.

That so few smugglers in the sample were familiar with smuggling through the Mexican border may be a function of the fact that many of them were arrested before Mexico was used as a mid-shipment point. It may also be that the word about the opportunities for using Mexico had not gotten out until after these smugglers had been convicted. Those who were familiar with Mexican routes mentioned that they had heard that the poverty and potential for corruption of police and government officials in Mexico made moving drugs through the Southeast border a profitable option.

Summary

A number of important insights were provided by the smugglers during discussions about transportation routes and methods. The first is that there are multiple routes available to smugglers seek-ing to bring drugs into the United States, offering organizers am-ple opportunity to vary routes to avoid detection. Of note is the response to interviewer questions about the easiest and most diffi-cult points of entry into the United States. The smugglers identi-fied the Mexican border as among the easiest because of its size and the potential for corruption, and also any point of entry on the water, especially when using private vessels, because of the vol-ume of other traffic on the water. They identified airports and commercial shipyards as the most difficult, because both are much more regulated and are limited in terms of options and opportu-nities to shift approach midcourse than are other points of entry.

The smugglers were also able to provide a significant amount of detail about methods used to smuggle drugs using private ves-sels, providing insight on why methods have shifted and how transporters try to avoid detection. It is clear that the current use of sophisticated compartments has had a significant impact on smuggler perception of risk. Despite the fact that more people are needed to organize these kinds of operations, larger loads are involved, and boats must be transported to a warehouse to be of-floaded (all of which should increase associated risk), smugglers expressed a sense of immunity to detection. The reasons are the difficulties associated with detecting drugs while on board (which is the best opportunity for detection, since the majority of U.S. assets are on the water), the reluctance of law enforcement to damage an expensive boat in search of drugs, and experiences of being boarded by law enforcement with no detection of the drugs. Detection difficulties when dealing with compartments are real and highlight the importance of further use of confidential infor-mants and cooperating defendants to learn about smuggling op-erations instead of trying to detect drugs on the water.

Smugglers did not describe much variety in the methods used to transport drugs over time. Most of the smugglers were boaters and changed the type of boat and specifics of the method of storage in response to law enforcement tactics, but they still relied on boats. This suggests a degree of consistency within the smuggler community that may be used to the advantage of law enforcement. For example, recognizing that the volume of smuggling through vast waterways and ports may remain the same, emphasis may be better focused on cooperation of mid-shipment countries and the use of warehouses to unload the drugs.

Smuggler responses also point to the success of U.S. efforts to deter smugglers from flying drugs into the United States. Smugglers commented on tactics used by the United States and the ease with which planes are detected, which limited options on how to get drugs into the United States and further encouraged the use of boats to pick up loads dropped by planes at mid-shipment points. Finally, smugglers confirmed the difficulties associated with smuggling drugs using commercial boats and planes, citing the additional burden associated with organizing and executing these types of operations and, with respect to commercial planes, the minimal rewards (because only small loads can be brought in at one time).

These insights provide useful information for law enforcement, some encouraging and others discouraging. It is encouraging that tactics implemented to deter planes from flying drugs into the United States have been successful and that conditions inherent in commercial airports and shipyards limit the degree to which smugglers consider commercial airplanes and containers viable methods of bringing drugs into the United States. The biggest obstacle presented by the smugglers is controlling the use of private vessels to smuggle drugs, particularly vessels with sophisticated compartments. Law enforcement must come up with better ways of identifying irregularities on water, but more importantly must focus on the complications added by compartments (larger crews, the need to transport boats to warehouses, and the use of warehouses to extract drugs from the boat). Also of concern is the perception that the Mexican border is an easy point of entry into the United States. This observation is worth further exploration, given the limited direct experience with the Mexican border by the smuggler sample.

5 Roles, Recruitment into, and
Remaining Involved in the
Drug Smuggling Trade

n this chapter, we introduce the various roles the smugglers
played in operations and the way each became involved in the
drug smuggling trade. These conversations allowed us to identify the way individuals are recruited, the way roles evolve over
time, and reasons for continued involvement, including smuggler's perceptions of that involvement. In these conversations, we
were trying understand how people become involved in the trafficking business, how individuals participate in an operation and
the various roles they can fill, and why people stay involved over
time.

To collect information on specific roles in the smuggling trade,
we asked smugglers about their involvement in the operations for
which they were convicted. Three smugglers maintained their innocence and said they were involved only because they talked to
someone and, therefore, became part of a conspiracy. Nine
claimed that, although they may have planned other smuggling
events or had been involved with the organization in other roles,
the offenses for which they were convicted were their first in-
volvements in the actual transport of drugs. Although these offenders were not able to describe careers as drug traffickers, they

did share information on the business of trafficking drugs based on their experiences in other aspects of the organization or through the experiences of their friends.

Twenty-two of the smugglers openly admitted to having been involved in smuggling drugs more than once. This figure compares closely with our review of presentence investigation information. In most cases, they began working for the organization as bodyguards, translators, offloaders, or delivery people and moved to transporting and then to managing transportation. Two acknowledged working for drug smuggling organizations, but primarily as money launderers, and although they were familiar with the operation, they had no direct experience of smuggling drugs into the United States. In a few cases, smugglers began working for the organization as accountants, gofers, or chauffeurs and claimed to have learned about the illegal aspects of the organization only after they began working in these capacities.

The majority began working in the smuggling business in the mid-1970s and had been in the business for between ten and twenty years before getting caught for their most recent offenses. They claimed involvement in anywhere from two and two hundred offenses, with an average of thirty-five. Almost all the smugglers were serving time for their first and only conviction for trafficking drugs. This makes sense; sentences are long enough to effectively remove them from circulation for quite some time.

We use the information provided by those who admitted to having been involved in multiple drug smuggling operations in the following descriptions of the various roles people play in the smuggling operation and the way smugglers are recruited into those roles and maintain their involvement.

Drug Smuggling Roles

It has commonly been observed about prison interviews that everyone reports having been a leader, a kingpin, or a shot caller.

We purposely included individuals at high levels in terms of the quantity of drugs they smuggled, the length of time they were involved, and their roles. Given the selection criteria, it is not surprising to find that most smugglers in our sample were in the upper echelons of drug smuggling. Most played significant roles in organizing the drug smuggling event, whether negotiating for the load, coordinating transportation, or securing contacts across transfer points in the transit and sale of the drugs. However, it is also important to note that they were involved in a range of roles and activities. In addition, roles could change for an individual over time or even within a single transport.

The key variable that distinguished two large categories of roles was contact with the drugs. There was a clear distinction between roles in which individuals had physical contact with or saw the drugs and roles in which there was no contact. The former category included roles of lower status, and the individuals in such roles were more susceptible to being caught. This group included offloaders, boat captains and crew, airplane pilots, and individuals involved in the warehousing and transport of the drugs upon entry into a U.S. port. An additional distinguishing feature between types of roles was contact with Colombians in the source country. Individuals who negotiated with and had contact with people in Colombia had higher status than those who never gained access to such contact.

Offloaders

A small number of individuals in our sample worked as offloaders, removing the drugs from the boats in which they were transported. These individuals were responsible for transferring the drugs from one mode of transportation to another or for providing storage for the drugs. They were the least sophisticated, though by no means the least important, smugglers. They had a greater risk of apprehension than did the people in any of the other roles because the drugs were in their possession in the United States, often under circumstances that created high anxiety about detection.

> I helped to unload it and I stayed with them for about one month to drive their car. (34)

> I had to make sure. My job was really to make sure the vessel reached the inlet in Tampa safely, you know? In other words if it would have got caught, it would have been on them [those responsible for off loading the dump]. Mine was just to make sure the boat, you know, got there and make sure no other boat would get close to it. My job was again security, and as soon as the drugs came in, I was to grab hold of the load and put it in the truck and leave with another pair of trucks guarding me to make sure I got into Miami with the product. (4)

> We supposed to be—we took the merchandise on the boat, you know. Drive the boat to the yacht, give the stuff to the people, and we go back to Bahamas, to Nassau. (14)

> I'm supposed to be the person that is going to pick it up from the freighter and bring it into Florida shore. (7)

Boat Captains

A large number of individuals in our sample were involved in the boating business. We interviewed a boat owner who himself was not involved in the actual smuggling of the drug, but instead had others drive his boats. A more common role was to serve as the captain or driver of the boat. In almost all instances, the captains had a solid working knowledge of the seas and of boating patterns in the Caribbean, plus the ability to engineer hidden compartments in their boats. They rarely had to advertise their skills;

a large network of individuals in South Florida watched for people with such skills.

> I do the transportation. (32)

> I mean you make a boat [put together a load of drugs]. You call me because I'm a good captain. You know what I mean? (25)

> I was just a delivery person. I had [my] boat reconfigured. I engineered all the little particulars like they'd call on the phone, the warehouse and the codes for everything. (12)

> [My job was] To leave from Miami and go to the Bahamas and pick it up. I'd leave—once the drugs would reach the island, a couple of days later, I'd leave. (22)

> They call me the leader because I'm the one who carry the drug on the boat, but I'm just an instrument working for them for the transportation. I do freight. (2)

Airplane Pilots

We interviewed relatively few individuals who served as airplane pilots in drug smuggling activities. Such individuals were able to transition from legal to illegal activity quite easily. One individual found it easy to move from a supportive to a lead role, suggesting that the learning curve for moving from underling to organizer or transporter might not be very steep, and that movement up and down the organization was not that difficult.

> I smuggled [with] small aircraft, DC-3, and we smuggled—six trips of five thousand kilos—five hundred pounds of weed. They trust[ed] you know, everybody trust one another. You have to have the equipment, and you tell them I have

this, I have that. I help—well, I help a few ships. Afterward I
go for myself. I had knowledge of the sea. I never bring it in.
I remain clean all the time. (33)

Organizers

A number of individuals in the sample had experience in organizing the transportation component of several drug smuggling
ventures, typically from mid-shipment points to the United
States. By and large, these individuals shared a number of characteristics. First, they were familiar with multiple stages of the
operation, a characteristic rarely found in most of the other roles,
which had discrete boundaries. Second, they had longer tenures
of involvement in drug smuggling; rarely had they smuggled only
a couple of loads. Third, almost all had contacts with Colombians, in Colombia, in South Florida, in both locales. Finally,
these individuals had access to multiple methods of transportation. If a role can be called central to drug smuggling operations,
it is the role of the organizers.

I know the whole operation from making the drug to delivering the drug. I was a transporter, I never owned the merchandise. (31)

Airplanes, boats, logistics, everything it has to do to get there.
Transportation is one thing, okay? That office in Colombia is
supposed to get the people in Miami to do the smuggling,
right? And I was the head, you know, my own group. Got
twenty people working for me doing the smuggling, ten people, whatever and that is my responsibility. They [in Colom-
bia] got nothing to do with that. (29)

I went to Colombia with [that guy]; he was a fugitive from
this country, and I was in charge of, in here, to make all of
the arrangements and all of the preparations . . . everyone
get his part and I get mine. (18)

I'm the transport. I'm the one that tells them this is how we're going to play the game. We're going to do it this way. We're not going to use this. We're going to do this because I'm in charge and I'm aware of surveillance. I know everything how—how the government is running things, how things are happening. So I keep constant contact with the office. All the broker does is pick up the drugs and give me the money that I'm going to—for my services. (1)

In Colombia at that time I spotted planes of the loads. I go over there and spotted the freighters or planes or anything. [Later] I took any class of transportation. I had the freighter, I had the boat, I had the plane. (3)

U.S. Brokers and Intermediaries

Other individuals served as contacts or intermediaries. Their function was to act as go-betweens, brokering for goods, services, or personnel. Many performed very important roles. In some cases, they were responsible for laundering the money, about which very little is known both by others involved in smuggling and by the authorities. Disposing of large sums of money can be as difficult as disposing of large quantities of drugs, particularly since the former is regulated and audited heavily.

Truthfully, in this one, as far as the drugs, nothing. Yes, I was in charge of the money laundering. (6)

I got involved in money laundering. I knew a guy that was giving me cash, and we was giving him checks. At that time it wasn't a big deal. (8)

In other cases, these individuals provided warehouse space or personnel. Often their roles involved little more than making a contact or ensuring that a plane or boat would be met. Yet, despite their comparatively low levels of involvement, such individuals often were charged with large roles and high-level offenses by the government, reflecting their importance to the drug smuggling enterprise.

> You see, it's like in any small business. Sometimes you are the only person there. Your duties won't be completely limited to accounting. You may have to do some driving or something like that, which I would do. Usually, a lot of times I'd get stuck in the so-called safe house or the warehouse. Someone has got to control the inventory, keep track of what goes out and what comes in. That would be my job. (24)

> My involvement was to meet the guy in New York. I would meet him outside, and he would give it [the dump] to me. Whatever came through, I would take it from there. I would be out there before the flight arrived and when he gets there the guy knows me, I know him. He hands me everything, and then I'm gone. (27)

Recruitment into Drug Smuggling

This section of the chapter documents the drug smugglers' responses to questions about the process by which they became involved in drug smuggling. Involvement occurs at two levels: recruitment into the initial act of drug smuggling, and recruitment into subsequent smuggling activities and new roles. Where available and appropriate, we make such distinctions in our findings.

Our use of the term *recruitment* implies a formal, purposive effort to involve others in an activity. As such, this term may overstate the formality of organizations and ignore the more dominant role of routine everyday activities that create relationships. Ianni (1974) observes that relationships in criminal organizations can be founded on personal ties or on organizational ties. Most of our subjects got involved in drug smuggling because of their friendships with or relational links to individuals already involved in smuggling. Indeed, the pattern of everyday life—which includes contact with or bonds to blood relatives, affiliational ties with workers or neighbors, or links to persons who can perform reciprocal favors—works to create opportunities for recruitment into drug smuggling. After all, it is unlikely for a stranger to be approached on the street and asked to assist in a drug smuggling effort.

We found little evidence that individuals were recruited "cold" for the specific skills they could bring to drug smuggling efforts. That is, none of our respondents told us that they recruited a boat captain or a money launderer who was unknown to them when they needed such an individual (or that they were recruited that way). People appear to be recruited through a process of large networks, where typically they are known to others through means other than drug smuggling. This process underscores the informal elements of trust and word of mouth that work in most drug smuggling networks. This resembles a small family business more than a large corporate environment.

One variable that did distinguish the recruitment of some individuals was their acknowledgement that their prior involvement in drug smuggling was part of the reason for their recruitment. Such individuals were likely to acknowledge their criminality and accept responsibility for their actions. On the other hand, many individuals became involved without explicit knowledge of their complicity in drug smuggling, particularly because it was their first event.

Personal Ties

Individuals are often recruited through ethnic ties. This is particularly true among Colombians, who are more likely to trust another individual of Colombian ethnicity than to trust members of other ethnic groups. Similarly, Cubans were much more likely to recruit and trust other Cubans, particularly for activities related to boats and the tasks associated with loading, shipping, and offloading drugs. This was especially true of Colombians and Cubans in the

Miami area. For example, a Colombian in Miami trusted and involved another individual based on word from the home country.

> I have a good position. I have good career. I have my wife and everything you know, but I was trusted because the person that [I knew] in Colombia were the leaders of the organization. They trusted me because they saw my job, more experience you know. I live in Colombia, my family lives in Colombia. (23)

One smuggler estimated that 90 percent of Colombians are involved in the drug trade and the other 10 percent are connected through relations.

> [L]ike if you say Colombian. You look at a Colombian; you're going to think about drugs right away. (22)

Poverty in Colombia may drive this. The profit achieved on a coca crop in contrast to any other type of crop planted by South American farmers is compelling.

> The people in the higher classes are basically, one way or the other, assumed to have done it [smuggling] at one time or presently doing it to get what they did get, to have what they had. (6)

The fact is that poverty makes people vulnerable to involvement in illegal activity. In many cases, such as drug smuggling, this involvement becomes a primary means of survival and an acceptable way of making money.

> In Colombia, the war against drugs has solved big problems for a lot of people that are starving to death right now. Let me tell you what happens. There's a guy that has three children and a wife. He can't send the children to school because there's no money. He can't work because there's no work.

He's starving. He's living in space about this big with three
children and—somebody comes to him and says, "Look, I
want you to get in this boat, and this boat is going to have
five thousand pounds of marijuana. You might get caught,
okay? And you are going to do five years in prison. . . . I'm
going to give you $10,000 right now. With $10,000 your
family is going to be supported like kings and queens for a
year. . . . If you are caught, you will be working in Unicorp
[a prison industry]. . . . And then you are going to make—
you're going to clear a month at least $300. . . . If you clear
you make another $10,000—that's $20,000. If you don't we
will support your family and in five years you come back." If
he is caught, they don't follow through, but this is the situation in Colombia. (13)

Unfortunately, this represents the way drug traffickers protect
themselves when they recruit others; they put the families of low-
level participants between themselves and the recruits. If the person solicited to work gets caught and becomes a government
witness, his family will be in jeopardy for retaliation.

Relatives were also a source of recruitment, and many individuals depended on brothers, cousins, and children as a ready
source of trusted employees who could reliably be brought into
the smuggling enterprise. Many smugglers expressed the belief
that they were less likely to be "snitched out" by relatives.

So my cousin, a distant cousin of mine, asked me for a job,
and I said, "Yes, I might find you a job in construction." He
said, "No I want to make some money." I said, "Well if I was
in that business one thing for sure I will do is that I do not
work with family." I had a barbecue at my house. He insisted
again. I said, "Well, you want a job go talk to that guy." (13)

Friendship provided a large number of contacts for new
sources of labor. The deeper or more long-standing the friendship, the more the person was regarded as being safe to hire.

Most smugglers viewed the people they worked with as the greatest threat in terms of being caught. They trusted their co-smugglers with their lives in many instances, and with millions of dollars in almost every smuggling event. Choosing associates was an important task, one not to be taken lightly.

> If a person were going to start out and do it independently, I would imagine that the hardest part would be getting a connection to actually bring the drugs in, to establish some credibility so that they would be trusted enough to be turned loose with millions of dollars worth of cocaine to come with it and do the trip. (12)

The absence of relational or ethnic ties meant that potential employees had to be closely scrutinized.

Sometimes friendship was the product of a lifelong relationship with a childhood friend, but in other cases it was the consequence of an intermediary who vouched for the person or put the two individuals together.

> You work for—references. Who you worked for, who had worked for you, you know. So you get to tell, look, I work for so and so and so, and usually, you know, everybody knows everybody. They will talk to each other. They say, "Yeah, he's good, he's bad." (29)

In most instances, the existence of friendship was not enough to secure a role in smuggling. Individuals had to have the reputation of being "straight"; a straight person was someone who could be trusted, who was not likely to bend under pressure, and who maintained that reputation in the community.

> [Question: Why did they come to you if you had never been involved before?] Because there was—the woman was a friend of mine, supposedly. I actually knew them because grew up with them. I mean, yeah, the same city. (26)

Well at first it was me and a friend, we used to go and bring in two or three [kilos]. (27)

Then in the middle of all these things arrived a guy that I know from my childhood in Colombia and said [name deleted], "I'm working in Miami with a person, like that, and that, and that, and that, because I don't know anything." I am not interested in that because I don't know him, I said, so he insisted that the persons that I would import for, they are in something. I had a good friendship with one of the persons that administered a storehouse, and I told him you talk to this guy. (20)

Well it was mostly based on friendship. (19)

Organizational Ties

The routine activities of everyday life create the largest source of contacts for recruiting individuals into drug smuggling. As a consequence of being involved in activities that include some aspect of the smuggling enterprise, individuals move from legitimate activity into, and sometimes out of, drug smuggling. Prominent among such activities are involvement in boating and the import business.

It is impossible to overemphasize the role of boating in the Miami area, in particular, in recruiting drug smugglers. Boat ownership is almost as common as car ownership in Miami, and people involved in various aspects of the boating enterprise often become known to each other. Conversations at marinas, at boat launches, on fishing expeditions, in boat shops, and at docks, as well as chance meetings on the water, can all lay the groundwork for relationships that can blossom into opportunities for involvement in drug smuggling. Involvement in an import-export business is also a means of recruiting other individuals into drug smuggling. Miami is the largest U.S. city proximate to Central and South America as well as to the Caribbean. As a consequence, there are a large number of import-export businesses in the area, and most of the businesses have warehouses and import goods on a regular basis.

Involvement in boating and in an import-export business provides expertise in many elements required for successful drug smuggling: legitimate cover, contacts, and the technology necessary to be successful. Other activities also provide opportunities, though their connection with smuggling is less direct. Many opportunities are a consequence of engagement in legal routine activities, such as working at an auto body repair shop, for a boat construction company, in a bakery, or in tailoring pants. This suggests the existence of widespread availability of drug smuggling opportunities in South Florida and also suggests that involvement can be initiated without much difficulty.

Fishing and boating were key activities for the smugglers we interviewed to move from otherwise legitimate activities to drug smuggling. Their knowledge of the sea, of boats, and of the patterns of boats on the sea made them likely targets of recruitment efforts. In many instances, as the quotations below demonstrate, recruitment did not require much in the way of coercion. The transition from legitimate activities was made easily. This presents challenges to law enforcement's attempts to advertise deterrents to involvement in smuggling.

I had been going over to the Bahamas for many, many years looking for sunken Spanish treasure. I am a treasure hunter. My name having been referred to him as somebody who was very trustworthy and knew his way around in the Bahamas, and he called me up and he said, "I need you to drive a boat for me." (12)

My first venture in drugs was about when I was about nineteen years old. I used to fish off Miami River with my cousin, and I had a nineteen footer vessel. It was meant for fishing, and I was hired by some local fishermen to go out, follow route, and pick up a load of about—it was about five bales of marijuana. I didn't even know it was marijuana at the time [I was hired]. (16)

They were yeah. I didn't know it at the time, but by hindsight, I'd know, yes, they were [drug dealers]. Yeah, yeah. I started by doing their books [as an accountant] and through doing that tax return I started picking up other little jobs, go here and get a cashier's check or go here and deposit money or go here and meet this fellow or lease a building or things of that sort, gofer-type things. (24)

So this guy was in the store next to us, and we joke. You know, he would joke with me, right? You know, when you joke, it's like a little thing, you know, like not for real, but just in case I'm kidding you know? They wanted some favors done. That was it. I started working as a translator. And I started meeting people, and you know, you learn. I started doing my own stuff. The word gets around. You know, like everybody you are asking, they will tell you, "This guy is good." (29)

I was working in a body shop making no money. I'm busting my behind here working, and I'm making little money and you're driving a brand new car. What are you doing? He says, "You sure you want to get involved?" I said, "Hey with that type of money I sure want to get involved." That is how it started. (32)

While most of the subjects did not have prior arrests for offenses other than drug smuggling, by and large they were involved in other offenses. (This information became available in qualitative research; it would have been missed in a study of official records.) Involvement in other crimes often led to involvement in drug smuggling. It is easier to move from one illegal activity to another than it is to initiate the first criminal activity.

Some illegal activities served as natural gateways into drug smuggling. Most prominent among such activities was money laundering.

I started working for other people that were in the business doing money laundering. I was doing this business for about three years, and then I stopped to do legal businesses and change my lifestyle. But then this situation started at the end of 1987 till 1991. (30)

I got involved in money laundering. You know, I was—I knew a guy that was giving me cash, and we was giving him checks. At that time it wasn't a big deal. (8)

Other individuals who were already involved in illegal drug activities, either in their home country or as small sellers on the street, also made their way into the drug smuggling business.

I came over to Miami [from Colombia], and I already was involved in drugs and all of that, you know, using drugs. And I think I got involved with, you know in with the people who was in that thing. (18)

Well, I came specifically [from Colombia] to do the operation to do the . . . to receive the merchandise. (15)

Government Recruitment

The final group of individuals came to drug smuggling or were recruited for specific drug smuggling operations when the U.S. government tried to enlist them as confidential informants (CI). In one instance, an individual from the Mariel boat lift operation was recruited by the government because of his equipment and his experience in the Gulf of Mexico and the Atlantic Ocean.

Well, I was recruited by them [the U.S. government to be a confidential informant] because of all the equipment that I have, and one day, during the Mariel boat lift, I was asked by them if I will consider using my equipment and my men as an organization and, you know, they will be paying us, paying me $150, $200, $300 per trip, and I put everything into it. Through the different trips, I mean, when you start working with the Colombians, it's a chain reaction. You do the first trip, which is the hardest one, and then once they start having the confidence in you, they just call you and say, "Hey, we are ready to do one next month," and you get all of your stuff together, and you are ready. (22)

In other cases, individuals became confidential informants through their involvement in and arrest for drug smuggling.

A CI hired me. I mean the CI came from knowing a longtime friend of mine. I came, and this operation started like this. I didn't know these two people. This person, the CI, went to this other person that I don't know in New Jersey. This is a chain, the other one took him to my friend, and my friend brought him to me. (9)

Because this guy, the CI, he is my friend, and he woke me up in the middle of the night. I don't know he was in jail before. (2)

Motivation for Drug Smuggling

The next few sections describe the motivation for continuing to be involved in drug smuggling operations, the way roles might shift over time, and personal perceptions of involvement over time. It is commonly presumed that the motivation for involvement in crime is monolithic. That is, most observers infer that the single reason individuals become involved in crime is to make money. However, this assumption has been called into question by recent research. Extensive interviews with active residential burglars (Wright and Decker, 1994), armed robbers (Wright and Decker, 1997), and crack sellers (Jacobs, 1999) have demonstrated that although money was a primary motivation for involvement in crime, it was not the only motivation, and it was not always the most important motivation. We found this to be the case among the smugglers we interviewed. Keeping up appearances, maintaining a party lifestyle, and acting in concert with friends and relatives often served to motivate these individuals to engage in crime. However, the money, the lifestyle it affords, and to a lesser extent the rush from not getting caught helped maintain their involvement.

> You know sometimes when you get a lot of money you cover your eyes and you don't want to see. (31)

Where else can a person make this type of money—particularly make it in a way that seems so easy? Some of the smugglers compared their legitimate earnings as pilots or fishermen with the amount of money they made in an hour or two of smuggling.

> I didn't—you know, once you got into it, it's not a matter of how long you're going to do it or what you're going to do, you know. Just at that time, you were making $400,000 [smuggling drugs] as a pilot then—well, now pilots get paid $200,000 or $300,000, but at that time, a pilot makes $10,000, $20,000, $30,000 at the most. (28)

Learning the Ropes

What was clear from the smugglers was that changing one's role and moving through the organization was more a function of trust than of skill. Some skill was, of course, involved, depending on the person's role. For example, boat captains and pilots were recruited for their skills and had to complete at least one successful run before they were able to market themselves as able transporters who could be trusted. But becoming a manager of the transportation was a function of contacts, which were established by generating trust and by word of mouth. Transporters could not operate on their own until they gained the trust of the Colombians. Many of the smugglers indicated that they stayed with the person who recruited them until they had enough contacts to function on their own. The transporters wanted to work on their own for independence and more money.

The Colombians employed a few tactics during the early phases of a new person's involvement. First, they tested the route the transporter was offering by sending a small load. The Colombians might also send a member of their group to monitor the operation, prevent potential theft, and testify to any problems encountered during the transport.

It did not take any of the smugglers long to become independent. As discussed earlier, they had usually been recruited on the basis of trust, word of mouth, or skill and experience. One smuggler noted that the Colombians could not afford to bring transporters up to speed slowly by giving them small loads and then progressing to bigger loads; a transporter was either in or out. None of the smugglers mentioned a long-term learning process or a system of establishing trust, generally because they were hired with a certain amount of trust already. Because their careers were based on contacts and reputation, they had to conduct business honorably.

> If you are in the business, you can trust that you are working with serious people. [It is] easy to get involved because know people and easy to get away with it. (21)

The smugglers' relationships with Colombian groups did not appear to be short term, particularly since they were built on trust and honor.

> When you start working for the Colombians, it's a chain reaction. It's like an assembly line, you know? You do the first trip, because it is the hardest one, and then once they start having the confidence in you, they just call you and say,

"Hey we're ready to do one next month," and you just get all your stuff together and you're ready. (22)

Once a smuggler was accepted by the Colombians and became a transporter or manager of transport, a crew often needed to be hired. Most smugglers mentioned doing the hiring through their own contacts in the business—often based on the culture-specific roles of the business. For Colombians these roles often included import-export activities or warehouse businesses that were traditionally associated with Colombian trade. As a general rule, though, almost all the smugglers who discussed recruiting mentioned that the crew members had to be recommended; they would not hire people who did not come to them through a contact. However, one smuggler mentioned that he hired his crew by talking to people who came through his boat shop.

Relationship to Street Drug Sales

Only six smugglers in the sample reported that they never used drugs themselves, while two admitted smuggling to support an addiction. Of the rest of the smugglers, six reported regular use of marijuana and cocaine on more than an occasional or social level. Smuggling was a means to get money, but not a means to get drugs. This is interesting because one of the smugglers who admitted to regular use said the following:

> Most of the people—I think 90 percent of the people who are in this business, they use drugs. And when you use drugs, your mind thinks quite differently than when you are not. And you think about some kind of—you think you are superior to other people, and you think that you know everything and all of that. (18)

A few of the smugglers were quite open about never having been involved in street drug sales, and they considered such sales to not be part of the business. Many did not link their activities to the street until they went to prison. Two of the smugglers also justified their actions by stating that they moved marijuana only because, morally, they felt marijuana was better than cocaine. For example, one smuggler said:

> You see it different. When you are smuggling, like I was . . . You don't see the damage that drugs do to people because you only deal with classy people, you know? You're rich and everybody around you is rich. You never see nobody smoking crack. You never see somebody stealing. You live in a nice neighborhood, you know what I mean? You don't see yourself like a drug dealer. You see yourself like a businessman. You didn't carry a gun. You didn't shoot nobody. . . . You shake your hand and that's honorable. (32)

Others said:

> I never sold on the streets, never. I mean, you know, I guess myself, there's a class. I am a businessman. (29)

> Organizing and touching drugs is lower-class work, I am a businessman. (15)

The impact of drug use, for example, never crossed the smugglers' minds.

> No, it's business. The guy is doing it, and I'm doing this for this amount of money, and that's all. He's not thinking about who's going to smoke that or who's going to die or who's going to do that. I mean, it doesn't even cross his mind. (13)

> A person is only thinking of the money without thinking of the consequences and tragedies it brings along. (720)

That's why I never had problems with the police or the authorities, because I didn't distribute it on the street, and I wasn't the owner of the drugs. (30)

Although many of the smugglers claimed to be unfamiliar with the distribution of drugs on the street, they were all involved in the distribution of drugs to the wholesaler for street-level dealing. They all knew how much a kilo of cocaine went for in the city in which they were working, and they factored that price into their transportation fee and the portion of the load to be held or to be given to them to cover transportation costs.

Leaving Drug Smuggling

In almost every case, smugglers did not seem inclined to leave smuggling until they had experienced prison for a length of time. Two mentioned that the loads they were caught with were going to be their last loads. Only one smuggler indicated that he might go back to smuggling after his release, and three smugglers mentioned wanting to work for the government as confidential informants.

One smuggler had even been caught before and went right back into smuggling because it was hard for a person with a conviction to get a job. He now felt that the lengthier sentence he received this time made him want to avoid getting involved again. However, smugglers find it difficult to separate themselves from the drug smuggling culture and lifestyle, especially when they are elderly men with convictions. As one smuggler put it:

Very few people retire from drug smuggling because once you get your first million, then you want five million, you want ten million. Greed, you know? Many people get out, but then they come back in because the money is so easy. (31)

Smugglers who claimed to be finished with the business said that the rush was no longer there and that smuggling was no longer fun because they knew they could get away with it (despite currently being in prison). Most also felt that the money was not worth the risk anymore.

> You get old and realize you can make same amount of money doing something else. Can't afford to go to jail anymore. (32)

Many agreed that they could not afford to go to prison again, either because another sentence would mean that they would die in prison or another prison stay would further the harm that their current sentences have already caused their families.

> They [the U.S. government] take everything from me. They leave so much time that they break you. You lose your family. You lose everything. (33)

> Not get involved narcotics again because all I got from that is pain. You know. Yes, one can make a lot of money, but it is not worth it; freedom is priceless, especially at my advanced age. (9)

Finally, it seemed that a number of smugglers realized that the negative effects of drugs are bad, and they did not want to contribute to the impact of drugs on U.S. society anymore. As one smuggler put it:

> A person does it only thinking about the money, without thinking about consequences and tragedies that it brings along. Now I realized that this is not good. (2)

The smugglers who were most emphatic about this epiphany had participated in a five-hundred-hour drug treatment program in the prison that covers the effect of drugs like cocaine and crack on the individual and society. One smuggler mentioned that he thought all the convicted smugglers and drug dealers should go through this program so that they too could appreciate the consequences of their actions.

Summary

It is important for law enforcement to understand the way smugglers are recruited into the business. When the smuggling operation was run by cartels, it was seen as well organized and efficient. With the demise of cartels and the separation of responsibility, the operation is less centralized and involves more entities. This, along with the use of confidential informants and cooperating defendants by U.S. law enforcement, has made trust a more important element of the job.

> It was easier to be accepted then. It was a smaller group and people knew each other a little bit better. (5)

Our study confirmed that smuggling networks are built on trust relationships with people already actively involved in smuggling drugs and on a combination of ethnic or familial ties, close friendships, and routine recreational or professional activities important to smuggling operations (e.g., boating and import-export businesses). It also confirmed that drug smuggling organizations seem willing to cross cultural lines when it involves business. As methods of transporting drugs began to expand, the ethnic makeup of the transportation groups began to diversify, with American military veterans flying drugs into the United States, Colombians negotiating with Cubans to airdrop loads off Cuba, and Bahamians securing landing strips in the Bahamas. This diversification increases risk, creating trust and responsibility issues. Another result is that Colombians limit their contact with the transportation groups and hold the managers of the transport responsible for the actions of their crews. This information is important to law enforcement attempts to infiltrate these organizations, perhaps encouraging more use of confidential informants with existing ties to the smuggling community by relationship or trade.

Our interviews also helped identify the various roles in smuggling networks, the information known by individuals in particular roles in the enterprise, and the identity of the roles that are more likely to generate information about the leaders of the distribution networks in the United States and the source countries. A recurrent theme is the dearth of formal organization that characterizes most of the drug smuggling activities our informants told us about. The lack of permanence, structure, and information flow across stages of the drug smuggling enterprise described by Williams (1998) and Griffith (1997) are consistent with most of the descriptions of roles we heard from our informants. Often an individual works in a small cell and has no contact outside a small circle of four or five people. In many respects, drug smuggling is big business that involves millions of dollars, affects the lives of millions of citizens, involves the activities of governments and government agents, and requires considerable coordination across different functions. Nevertheless, drug smuggling roles resemble those of small, family-owned businesses more than corporate hierarchies; the process often depends on word of mouth and ethnicity as entrees to the business rather than on technical qualifications (Williams, 1998).

Also noteworthy are the smugglers' perceptions of the easiest and hardest roles in the smuggling trade, which correspond to their perception that risk increases closer to the drug and its entry into the United States. The smugglers agreed that the hardest and most risky roles are those of "the little guys," the individuals at the end of the distribution chain who are involved in offloading, storing, transporting, or carrying the drugs in the United States.

The hardest role is the little guy. The little guy has the hardest role. He is the one that's got the pressure. You know, if he doesn't come through, he loses out on everything that he has dreamed of, big money, fancy cars. (6)

The United States. That's where the main risk is. (16)

Although there was less agreement, it was clear that the smugglers perceived that being an organizer, especially an organizer who does not leave Colombia, is one of the less risky roles.

The easiest is the head guy. He's never seen, and if he is seen, he's only seen by people in the upper echelon. (6)

The one that organizes this, the people that are unknown, the ones who finance this. The sponsors. (26)

The best job to have. Well the best job to have is to own the merchandise and be in Colombia, a safe place. That is the best job. (31)

Of most interest to law enforcement is the smugglers' impression of the vulnerability of the person at the lowest level in the organization, who is in direct contact with the drugs, and the relative security of the individual or network organizing activities in Colombia or another source country. In the next chapter, we explore how these perceptions affect strategies employed by smugglers to avoid detection and their attempts to balance perceived risks and rewards.

6 Balancing Risk and Reward

In our conversations with smugglers regarding methods, roles, and recruitment, it became clear that the smuggler community engages in a number of strategies to minimize risk and avoid detection. Some of the strategies appeared to be universal, while others were specific to the size of the load, the method of transport, and the transportation route. In this chapter we describe these strategies, their increasing importance after President Ronald Reagan declared his war on drugs, and how Reagan's war resulted in changes to the smuggling trade. We also introduce smuggler assessments of risk, the level at which a smuggler would be deterred from smuggling drugs into the United States, and how risk perceptions may alter as a result of a smuggler's experience with the U.S. criminal justice system.

Minimizing Risks

Smugglers have to focus on a number of things during the smuggling operation, including law enforcement, people ripping you off, snitches, equipment, time, thinking clearly, and not being nervous. To manage the risks, people involved in the business seem to live by a number of rules of the drug smuggling game.

Keep Your Crew Small

The number one rule for almost all smugglers is to keep the size of the crew small, for both practical and precautionary reasons. Eight to ten people are usually involved in organizing a load, but a crew may consist of only four members. Limiting the number of people involved in an operation reduces the chance of error because the size of the load is manageable, and the operation is less likely to get out of control. Smugglers balance this goal with the size of the crew required to successfully bring in the load.

> When you bring in a load, you use a lot of people, okay? You use people on the ground to secure and transport when it gets there. You use the boat and the bait to watch the cops. You use the guys in each boat, one loaded, one empty, to secure if the boat break down, you got another boat next to you to bring it in, okay? You use the people on the ground and in the Bahamas. (32)

> Once the load gets too big, it's—you need a lot of space to bring it in, and the boat, like the one I was using, doesn't—it doesn't have that capacity, and then, you know, you're using two boats. You're talking about four people that you got to control, you know, four boats—two boats that you got to make sure they're right all the time. It's a lot of responsibility. (22)

In addition to keeping crews small, many smugglers also either reduced their involvement in the transport or hired crews to organize each operation and limited their contact with the organizer of each crew.

Trust Your Crew

A small crew also limits the chance of involving members who are not well known by the other crew members and who, therefore, are not trusted—people who may become confidential informants or cooperating defendants if caught. As discussed in Chapter 5, when trying to recruit potential crew members, managers rely on word of mouth, reputation, and recommendations. They also look for people who have needed skills or equipment.

> When one has a certain activity, that activity takes you to another person that is involved in the same activity. (9)

> The word gets around. You know, like everybody you are asking, they will tell you, "This guy is good." (29)

> You know, a lot more people were cooperating with the government, and you didn't know who was who. So you wanted a small group. You wanted real trusting friends. (1)

> Because one good crew could cost you the load or go to jail. So you get tight with a crew. (29)

In addition to being trusted, it is also important for crew members to avoid posing a threat to the group by being flashy with proceeds, by getting drunk or high, or by doing anything else to make themselves unreliable or to call unwanted attention to themselves. The smugglers we interviewed discussed the importance of "being smart" with money to avoid suspicion. One of the tactics associated with being smart is using front operations to explain cash. At least nine of the smugglers mentioned having other jobs or businesses that would provide cover for their smuggling income. These businesses included a car dealership, a trucking company, a mechanic shop, a paint and body shop, a jewelry store, an import business, and even a fish market. Some of the businesses were just front operations, but others brought in legal income. As one smuggler put it, if you have a cash business, you just overstate receipts to launder drug money.

Other tactics used by smugglers to avoid looking too suspicious include depositing the money in the bank in other people's names, giving people cash and asking them to write checks, buying real estate, putting money in a bag in a safe deposit box, putting money through money exchange houses in the airport, and using groups that send money to Colombia for a fee. A few also claimed to be generous, buying people cars and houses and basically just throwing money away. Finally, a few mentioned spending the money to make sure their boats were in top shape with the best equipment and technology available. More smugglers appeared to spend at least some of the proceeds this way, since having poor equipment is one the few reasons for getting caught that smugglers can control.

I'll Tell You Only What You Need to Know

Another rule is for the smuggler to protect his identity in order to protect himself and his family. To this end, many organizers never let their Colombian connections know where they lived, never made calls on home phones, never used their homes as safe houses or as any other bases of operation. Similarly, information was provided to others in the organization only on a need to know basis, and this information was carefully filtered. Such filters applied to information passed to transportation managers by Colombian contacts as well as to information passed to the crew and the broker in the United States. At all levels of the operation, the cells responsible for different tasks were self-contained, and layers between the head of the cell and the actors below him acted as further protection. If someone got caught, he could not snitch on other components of the operation or on the person managing it.

Avoiding Detection

In addition to carefully selecting the crew and limiting information flow, smugglers took surveillance and precautionary measures very seriously, since the drugs were fronted to them and they were responsible for any part of the load that was lost. Two rules that all smugglers seemed to live by were to avoid being suspicious and do their research.

Avoiding Suspicion

Some of the techniques the managers we interviewed used to avoid suspicion included switching boats to prevent any one boat from getting "hot," maintaining an element of surprise by changing patterns or switching to an alternate method of transport or offload, and blending with other traffic by transporting during the busiest times (holidays and weekends). Other precautions included arriving at the rendezvous point early to supervise the exchange, scouting out a mid-shipment point before selecting it, flying over the pickup point in advance, and having a plan B, whether a second drop point or a return to the mid-shipment point. Managers also broke loads up at mid-shipment points to accommodate certain methods or to minimize loss. Only two smugglers with whom we spoke mentioned taking a weapon with them as protection, and they mentioned that they brought the weapon in reaction to piracy, not because of any law enforcement threat. Eight smugglers specifically stated that they did not carry weapons.

Do Your Research

Many of the smugglers talked about monitoring the activities of the Coast Guard and Customs and having someone on the inside feeding them information. Only a few smugglers said that they did not use surveillance, tracking, and detection equipment.

> When you're in this kind of business, you want to find out your odds, what kind of surveillance the government is using, what interdiction efforts. (1)

Many of the smugglers described their role as facilitating business. Just as in any other business, members monitored the market and shared information vital to the survival of the business. The drug smuggling business was not organized to effectively promote the sharing of information across groups or entities. Therefore, much information about interdiction activities was passed from group to group by informal means, such as word of mouth. Transporters exchanged information with other transporters and management teams in Colombia and the United States also exchanged information. Information sharing occurred before or after operations, during the planning of operations, and during operations, particularly if the smuggler worked for a group in Colombia. In all cases, however, collection of information did not seem to be done proactively; it seemed to be done more as a forewarning tactic. As a result, information tended to move in waves, and changes in the business did not occur as dramatic shifts, but rather more as evolutionary events.

Many smugglers felt that watching the news, reading the newspaper, and reading articles in Colombian papers gave them enough information to identify major interdiction efforts. They felt that the news media covered most things they needed to know. Two smugglers specifically mentioned two Colombian weekly newspapers, the *Semana* and *Cambio,* as useful resources about drug smuggling interdiction risks. Some also mentioned doing their own research on new surveillance techniques and equipment in case law enforcement began using something new.

Three smugglers specifically mentioned paying off U.S. law enforcement officials for information on interdiction and other activities. One talked about paying off U.S. federal agents to use an island off Colombia as a mid-shipment point. Another mentioned paying off crews at two U.S. airports. Corruption at mid-shipment points was also seen as common in Mexico, Cuba, and the Bahamas.

It is a common claim among people suspected of crimes that law enforcement "put a case on them" or otherwise engaged in illegal contact. These smugglers' views about law enforcement contacts were different than those expressed in the usual jail-house complaints about illegal police behavior.

> Eventually you meet people you might need, holding differ-ent positions [the reference is to officials in Puerto Rico and to Mexican policemen], and they don't know that you are do-ing illegal things. You have a friend, you have a relationship with someone, so you start asking questions and you start getting information. When you already trust that person then start to use him. I had some that I would pay and some wouldn't pay because they didn't want any money. (30)

Most of the smugglers felt that they did not have to resort to pay-ing off officials because information about shifts in interdiction strategies and tactics became public knowledge quickly enough for them to respond.

In general, information about U.S. law enforcement activities was not purchased, but instead was gathered through the use of spotters, lookouts, and such tracking tactics as using scanners and listening to law enforcement channels on the radio. Many smug-glers felt that simply identifying the location of enforcement boats was enough to avoid being surprised on the water. They also checked whether the radar balloon was up or down, programmed the radar on the boat to alert them to other boats within a certain radius, and merely looked out on the water if they were traveling during the day. Smugglers typically viewed their concern with law enforcement as reactive rather than proactive. As one smuggler succinctly put it:

> You ain't carrying a flag saying I'm a smuggler. (29)

When U.S. law enforcement groups put Operation Pulse or new surveillance technologies into practice, the smugglers reacted with sufficient speed by altering routes or changing methods to avoid capture. Most of the smugglers we spoke with had been smuggling during periods of changes in U.S. law enforcement tactics, and they mentioned changing their practices. The fact that they were not caught before changing suggests that their level of sophistication in intelligence gathering may not be great, but perhaps is sufficient.

State of Mind

In exploring subjects' state of mind during their drug smuggling operations, it must be recalled that in addition to the highly subjective nature of state of mind, subjects are recalling highly charged emotional experiences from many years earlier. We believe that the distinctive nature of the drug smuggling event, combined with its salience in the lives of these subjects, makes their responses less subject to memory loss than are more mundane issues.

Most subjects reported that their state of mind during the execution of a smuggling event was one of confidence. While conscious of the risks they were about to take, these individuals sought to put such thoughts as far from their minds as possible. This is important because the ability to think clearly in the face of pressure is an important characteristic of decision making. Sometimes the size of the potential gain helped the smugglers put the risks out of their minds, while other times smugglers pragmatically ignored the risks so as to better focus on the tasks at hand.

> Fear is not an option. You do not have the option of expressing fear when you are in the presence of a shark. If you do, you are going to become part of the food chain. I never even thought about it [getting caught]. I knew their planes and helicopters were faster than I am, but I never even suspected that they would even know where I was. The Bahamas are just so big. (12)

> [The risk didn't matter.] I didn't want the money to be rich or anything like that. I only wanted to bring my family to the United States. (34)

There's always risk, but the risk—if I'm going to say I'm going to make three million dollars and I know I'm broke—right now, if you ask me would I do it again, I would tell you no because of the suffering of my family. But very few people retire from drug smuggling because once you get your first million, then you want five million. You want ten million. Greed is the name of the game, you know? (31)

In other cases, two factors worked to neutralize risks: technology and experience. As noted earlier, a large number of the subjects we interviewed depended on technology at some point in the smuggling enterprise. Without exception, every member of our sample was aware of the use of radio, cellular phones, sophisticated communication devices, GPS, and radar in the tracking of U.S. assets. But the technology of smuggling was not simply a GPS device or radar used during a boat trip; it also involved the use of tools, expertise, and mechanized customizations to bring a load in successfully.

The largest alternative technological category was the building of secret compartments on boats. In many cases, the subjects were quite sophisticated in the construction of such compartments, and they went to great lengths to secure them from outside scrutiny.

I was 99 percent sure that law enforcement couldn't find the hidden compartment. But I didn't even know the penalty for bringing in cocaine. I thought if you were sophisticated enough and you had the right people, there was no limit to what you could [get away with]. (5)

I know machining techniques, planing, all that stuff. So I just put my expertise to work, and the vessel that I had, I felt like it was one of the best that there was. (12)

Although a few subjects were unlucky enough to be caught on their first smuggling ventures, most had considerable experience in the transport of illegal drugs into the United States. These experiences were vital to their preparations and their considerations of risk. For most, a successful first trip was the catalyst that set off a series of smuggling ventures.[1] Their experience helped them quell their fears and anxieties and balance the risks against the likely gain. Their initial experiences confirmed what individuals and conventional wisdom told them about the chances of being caught: that the waters are great, that the U.S. assets are relatively limited, and that boats and other conveyances get through all the time. Armed with these beliefs, they were emotionally free to set out on the drug smuggling enterprise.

> There is no way the United States can stop it unless they got somebody that tells them. I mean, they have a lot of planes out there. They have a lot of things, but there's always a way. There's no way the United States is going to stop it. When you're making money, your mind sometimes—you think you're indestructible. (8)

> I know the water. I know how things work, and it's just—there's a lot of water out there and you can't cover it all. I knew the government and law enforcement worked and how they set their surveillance, how they would do their interdictions and I always—I'd be a step ahead of them, and I knew that. (1)

Changes in Smuggling Activities in Response to Risk

Many of the smugglers referred to the "early days of smuggling drugs" as the time when the primary drug Colombia exported to the United States was marijuana and smugglers brought in boats with thousands of pounds of marijuana sitting on the deck. Many mentioned that law enforcement just did not care then and that there was no thought of hiding the marijuana in compartments.

In 1981 President Ronald Reagan declared a war on drugs, and law enforcement began to crack down on drug smuggling. Smugglers reacted by starting to use compartments, but the compartments were not sophisticated because the loads were too big. Smugglers had already switched to using boats to move the marijuana because the loads needed to make a profit were too big for airplanes. In about 1985 most smugglers began switching from marijuana to cocaine as a result of perceived increases in enforcement and because of economics. Cocaine was easier to bring in, and smaller loads would produce as much, if not more, money than did marijuana.

> The Colombians and a lot of Cubans won't mix cocaine and marijuana together. They think it's bad luck. They won't bring it in on the same boat. So eventually, some of the guys that I knew that were in the smuggling business were doing marijuana and some were doing cocaine, and they just eventually all changed over because it [marijuana] was so hard to hide. It just eventually all changed over to cocaine. (5)

Smugglers now had loads that were more manageable and that generated profits that were worth the risk. As the war on drugs continued, law enforcement pressure escalated, and smugglers continued to respond.

> I stopped in '87–88 because it was getting more difficult. You know, the boats—my cigarette boats were like, you know—it's like law enforcement already knew. I mean, a thirty-seven-foot Midnight Express with four engines in the back, they knew what the boat was for. So, you know, my—my operation was getting obsolete already. So, in the mid-'80s I switched to cocaine. I wanted to work with something that there was plenty of money and something that I could get in and out of and, you know, do my delivering fast, didn't have to use a lot of people. You know, a lot of people were cooper-

ating with the government and you did not know who was who. (1)

As noted previously, smugglers began building more sophisticated compartments and using containers in commercial freighters to hide the drugs. The interesting problem posed by both transitions for law enforcement was that the changes removed detection from the open water. This is important because U.S. assets are concentrated on the water. Boarding a boat with a sophisticated compartment or with two hundred containers while the vessel is in the water is not an efficient use of resources. Instead, suspected drug boats have to be taken out of the water and examined in dry dock. To target loads entering the United States in compartments or containers, law enforcement would have to focus on offloading procedures that often occur at private warehouses across the country.

With increased law enforcement pressure, some smugglers are converting to another, harder, drug that again promises more profit for a smaller load: heroin.

Sooner or later it is going to rebound for them. If you see, it went from pot to coke, from coke to heroin. So instead of going to soft drugs, we've gone to hard drugs because it's harder to bring it in. So you need to bring something that's more profit. (29)

Because it is more expensive, you make more money and it is easy to handle the quantities. There is not much volume. What you can earn with two hundred or three hundred kilos of cocaine, you can make it with eighty or one hundred of heroin. So it is easier to handle one hundred than three hundred. That's why I never worked with marijuana, because it was a big quantity. Although the sentence was less, now twenty-twenty hindsight it was better to be caught with marijuana. (30)

One smuggler talked about the shift from Americans' picking up loads to Colombians' transporting loads.

> If we [Colombians] don't bring drugs into U.S. the Americans will go to Colombia and get it themselves, like they did from the beginning. They started the whole drug trafficking. They are the ones who started it. They went to Colombia. They used to go with boats in Colombia, and they used to bring it to the United States. That's how the whole thing started thirty-five years ago. Maybe Americans are afraid they might get killed or kidnapped in Colombia or probably they are going to get robbed in Colombia. So it is easier for them. It's safe to stay here and buy the drugs in the U.S. That way don't have to risk their life going down there. (26)

What is important to note is that the shifts in smuggling were not dramatic but occurred in an evolutionary fashion as information filtered through different networks and across different roles. Just as information was not collected or transmitted in a systematic fashion, reactions to the information also did not occur systematically. Smugglers are dynamic; they can shift their tactics. As one put it:

> [W]hen Miami [got] too hot, then we went to Mexico off the Yucatan; now getting bad so [go] to Puerto Rico—so that's the game. We know when Coast Guard and Navy start increasing enforcement and just work around it. (31)

Some smugglers were looking ahead to the next major change in the drug smuggling market. In some cases, this included moving to Europe; in others, it meant changing transportation routes. In either case, there was not a good deal of advance planning.

> Put it this way, right now the United States is very—the market is lucrative, right? But the profit, it isn't there no more

like it used to be. Now, if you do your research and you look at all the countries, Australia, a kilo of coke goes for $8,000. Japan, it goes for $100,000. Now, I mean, like that's more money. The market is burned because people don't want to do the time. (29)

Getting Caught

Despite the research and precautions, all the smugglers we interviewed had been caught and were serving time in prison for conspiring to transport illegal drugs into the United States or for actually transporting them. Although three smugglers claimed that they were innocent of wrongdoing and nine claimed that they had been caught the first time they participated in planning or smuggling drugs into the United States (some had previously worked for the organization in other capacities), the remaining twenty-two smugglers admitted to having been involved in smuggling drugs.

Table 6.1 describes the way the smugglers were caught. It is interesting to note that almost three-quarters were caught through members of their crew, despite the care taken to recruit crew members and limit information sharing.

Among the seventeen smugglers caught through confidential informants working for the DEA or the U.S. Customs Service, six claimed that this was the first time they had been involved in smuggling, and one claimed that he was innocent. Two of the

TABLE 6.1   METHOD OF GETTING CAUGHT

	Smugglers	Percentage
Confidential Informant	17	50
Cooperating Defendant	7	21
Caught with Drugs	7	21
Undercover Operation	2	6
FBI Tip	1	2

seven caught through conversations between the government and cooperating defendants claimed that they were innocent and that the defendants lied. Another claimed to have been caught through a confidential informant and information provided by a cooperating defendant. Among the seven smugglers who were caught with the load, two said that this was their first offense and that they had very minor roles in the smuggling. One of the two caught through an undercover operation claimed it was his first offense, while the other claimed innocence. The last smuggler was a fugitive who was caught through a tip to the FBI. It is interesting to note that there were three fugitives in the sample.

The pathways to getting caught were rather straightforward and can be grouped into four categories: a confidential informant (CI) as part of a larger investigation, a snitch from inside the group, government surveillance, and an act of nature or mechanical breakdown.

Confidential Informant

Typically, a confidential informant is an individual who was caught by a law enforcement agency of the U.S. government who receives a consideration for reduction in his sentence in return for his cooperation. By far, confidential informants are more feared than are any other means of being caught. They are effective because they invade the security of the arrangements that allow smugglers to carry out the act of smuggling. In other words, confidential informants destroy the illusion (the state of mind) generated by trust and by working with individuals known to them that allows smugglers to minimize risks and execute the smuggling act. The use of confidential informants helps destroy their belief that they are safe and can trust their associates. This leads smugglers to take additional precautions that are costly in terms of time and money. As such, using confidential informants and fostering the belief that their use is widespread are powerful tools in combating drug smuggling.

Well, there was this American, the first to infiltrate the group. I don't know his whole name because he didn't want to go to trial. This man charged the federals $115,000 to turn us in. (34)

The CI heard from another fellow that I was bringing the load in, and he went and told the DEA. (5)

I wasn't that surprised [to get caught] because when you're in this kind of situation you go with two bags, one to lose and one to win. And I wasn't surprised when I was caught because as I told you before, I thought something was fishy because it was too easy to get that plane to land. (8)

Snitch from Inside the Group

Snitches in the group often function in the same way as confidential informants, but they usually operate at a lower level and often decide to cooperate once a group has been caught. These individuals often emerge in larger smuggling operations, where organizers or boat captains are less likely to know and have direct contact with individuals at the next stage of the smuggling process.

They named me to get themselves off the hook. They were being held by Customs. (6)

Because I think I should have kept the group small. I think I should have depended on myself, no on others, as I used to in the beginning. (22)

They got caught because they were stupid. How can you buy a $3 million house without a job? (32)

The only way I get caught is if you have somebody bad in your side or failures, equipment failures. (29)

Government Surveillance and Undercover Agents

Ironically, government surveillance and undercover agents receive the most public attention—and are the most expensive components—of efforts to curb the flow of illegal drugs into the United States. Despite this, the majority of smugglers we interviewed were far less fearful of these techniques than they were of confidential informants. Government surveillance leads smugglers to alter their routes, methods, or crews rather than capturing the smugglers in the act.

[Question: If you look back on it now, are there things that you see that should have made you suspicious?] Yes, for instance the way they [undercover agents] spend money. They were very cautious about spending money. Actually, we used to go to dinner or we used to go out and I was the one that was paying the bills. They didn't pay for anything. The way they were dressing, they didn't dress like the average drug dealer. They dress very shoddy. (28)

All of a sudden my gut said these are cops and they are going to put you in prison, and my other self said no, no, no, no you know. If you would walk into a bar and look around for the scroungiest, evilest looking person, that was the cop. They're sitting there with tattoos, with earrings, the leather jacket, hair. That's the cop. You could pick them out in a minute. (24)

I realized they were the Coast Guard when they were about a mile from me, by the way they were approaching going around. I had two options sink the boat or get caught. So I got caught. (2)

Act of Nature or Mechanical Breakdown

Sometimes things go wrong. This axiom applies to a variety of life circumstances, including drug smuggling. Boats run out of gas, break down, are late, and encounter unexpected contingencies such as storms or high winds. When this happens, the odds of being caught increase dramatically. A number of subjects could relate such experiences, most notably Subject 3.

> So he had a yacht, a sixty-eight footer, in Aruba at the time. So what he did, he loads the yacht and instead of sending to Holland he diverted. The boat breaks down out of Santa Domingo. The Coast Guard comes two days later to get the vessel. (31)

I Know I Am Not Innocent, but I Don't Like It

Most smugglers accepted the fact that they were doing something illegal and eventually would be caught, so they were not outraged when they were caught. They seemed to be more annoyed with law enforcement tactics than with anything else. It was almost as if they felt that the government cheated in catching them, particularly when they were charged with conspiracy or—even worse in their minds—a dry conspiracy.[2] Others who were new to smuggling or considered themselves retired before they were encouraged to get involved again were more annoyed with the new tools at the government's disposal. A few others felt that the process was flawed and that their trials were not fair because the juries were biased or their lawyers were inadequate or corrupt.

In discussions with the smugglers, it became clear that many thought that the only way they could be convicted was to have the drugs in their possession. Most were not aware of the options available to the government, specifically the use of the conspiracy clause and the ability to use confidential informants, and they felt that the tactics bordered on entrapment.

I'll tell you that there is a big difference between actually trying to do something and planning to do something. I'm extremely agitated, and I will be the remainder of my life, not because they caught me, or because I was doing something wrong, it's the method that they used. And that's the rat system [use of confidential informants]. (5)

Someone comes to offer you something and the guy is recording you while gaining your cooperation. At the moment you are talking to one of these guys, he is a criminal and he himself recorded the conversation. This is evidence for them, only by talking to the person is this a conspiracy (9)

What they [CIs] are in fact is crime creators in commission because they create scenarios that never would have otherwise existed had it not been for their involvement, and in this case the government's involvement. (24)

They were also not aware of the length of the prison sentences that could be levied on them.

Let's give an example. Right now you got a lot of people with life sentences. You got your twenty-five kilos. Let's say don't get life. Let's say they get twenty years in jail. They get out when they're forty-five. What do you expect them to do? What do you expect them to be? (28)

Even after being caught, almost all the smugglers felt that they would not be in prison if the government could not rely on intelligence gathering for making cold hits. They thought that they could not be convicted unless they were caught red-handed with the drugs. They were seriously uninformed.

The truth is that the way I think, if it wouldn't have been for these events and people talking about me, I think they would have never arrested me. (30)

Even when he knew DEA after him, he figured "Hey, I never touch the stuff. What can they do to me?" (29)

Nine were caught during what they claimed was their first smuggling offense. However, among the twenty-two who admitted to having been involved in smuggling drugs for a number of years, beginning in the 1970s and 1980s, only one had been arrested and convicted of smuggling before the current offense. Two others had been arrested before, but the charges had been dropped due to insufficient evidence or illegal search. Their prior success and their lack of knowledge about U.S. enforcement tactics fostered their sense of immunity and their perception of risk.

Assessing Risk

Drug smugglers operate by balancing risk against reward. We spent considerable time querying subjects about these topics. We attempted to have them discuss their perceptions of risk and reward for their first, a typical, and their most recent drug smuggling trips. It quickly became evident that sophisticated balancing of risks and rewards was well beyond the scope of most of our subjects. Risk was a constant, but its calculation was hardly representative of the "criminal calculus" suggested by rational choice or deterrence theorists. Instead, risk was present in any smuggling event, though its quantity was unknown, and in the end it had to be neutralized in some way in order for the smuggling event to take place. This neutralization typically occurred in ways that we discussed above (experience, expertise, or technology, for example), but it was critical to the decision to become involved in a smuggling event. We also learned that risk tolerance was dynamic, typically based on age and life stage concerns, including family, financial status, and status in the community.

A key element in the neutralization of risk was the magnitude of rewards. The lure of state lotteries and television programs such as *Deal or No Deal* and the attractiveness of get-rich-quick schemes on the Internet are well documented. The same processes were at work for the drug smugglers we interviewed, albeit at a considerably higher level. In the end, doubts were quelled with reference to the volume of reward awaiting them on successful completion of a drug smuggling event.

We found few individuals who remained involved in drug smuggling owing to their commitment to thrill-seeking lifestyles. However, nearly all our subjects could recount prior smuggling enterprises that included considerable thrills—thrills they missed while in prison. While pursuing a rush or a high was hardly the primary motivation for involvement, such pursuit was nonetheless a welcome attribute of drug smuggling and was an important part of the drug smuggling subculture. For those who remained in drug smuggling over a prolonged period of time (roughly ten years) and were assigned more responsibility for the loads, the calculus of a conservative businessman came to dominate.

One way we attempted to measure deterrence was to ask closed-ended questions that forced subjects to consider the potential effects of different levels of arrest, conviction, and incarceration. This proved more difficult than we anticipated. By and large, the subjects did not think of risks in terms of probabilities in the way that government agencies and social scientists do. Many could not conceptualize risk in the probability terms we asked them to use. For most, getting caught was simply one of two things that could happen when they smuggled drugs.

We began by asking subjects to think about whether they would continue to smuggle drugs into the United States if their chance of arrest was one out of one hundred, ten out of one hundred, or fifty out of one hundred. Fourteen subjects could not provide a direct answer to this question, illustrating their difficulties in addressing probability-based questions. Of those who did answer the question, none reported being deterred by a one in one hundred chance; 6 percent said that if the risk of arrest was ten in one hundred they would not offend; and 63 percent said that they would still offend if the chance of being arrested was fifty in one hundred. Clearly, risk of arrest had to be high in order to yield a deterrent effect. Because the gain was so high and experience told them that it was relatively easy to be successful, levels of arrest did not seem to be especially potent threats to deterring drug smugglers.[3]

Similar conclusions can be drawn from the analysis of the deterrent effect of conviction. Here we asked subjects about their decision to continue to smuggle drugs into the United States in the face of three different chances of being convicted: one in one hundred, ten in one hundred, and twenty-five in one hundred. Further illustrating the difficulty of utilizing such a calculus, only twelve subjects were able to complete this segment of the questionnaire. Not surprisingly, none would be deterred by the potential of a one in one hundred chance of being convicted, while all of the subjects would still offend with a ten in one hundred chance, and none would continue to offend with a twenty-five in one hundred chance. Clearly, the chance of conviction appears to be a more powerful deterrent than does arrest, and the tipping point for this is low.

We concluded this section of the questionnaire by examining the deterrent effect of prison terms. In this context, we asked about the deterrent effect of five-year, ten-year, and twenty-five-year sentences. Not one respondent indicated that a five-year sentence was sufficient to deter them from further involvement in drug smuggling activities. In the current configuration of U.S. Sentencing Commission guidelines, five years is no longer a realistic sentence for drug smuggling. Little deterrent effect was added by doubling this sentence to ten years; 75 percent of the subjects said that they would continue to offend if a sentence of this length awaited them on conviction. Interestingly, not one subject indicated that he would still offend if sentences were twenty-five years, a figure that corresponds closely to the average sentence received by members of our sample. The findings suggest that, at least for this group of high-level drug smugglers, twenty-five-year sentences have considerable deterrent value. The correspondence between this finding and the current level of sentences suggests an interesting opportunity for the U.S. government to produce more deterrence by widely publishing information about typical sentence lengths in regions of the country and the world that produce large numbers of drug smugglers. Mitigating the deterrent effect of sanctions are the large gains to be made, which often overwhelm a more rational deterrence calculus.

Perceptions of the U.S. Criminal Justice System

In addition to discussing levels of risk, we also discussed perceptions of the criminal justice process based on the smugglers' direct experiences. Specifically, we were interested in their perceptions of their capture, arrest, conviction, and sentencing, as well as of the way their experiences might affect their return to the drug smuggling trade.

Role of Arrest

The ability to neutralize the likelihood and the consequences of arrest was an important process for drug smugglers. At one level, they knew they were up against the collective power of the U.S. government, an awesome power indeed. On the other hand, most smugglers convinced themselves that the odds were in their favor, and of course for any single act of drug smuggling the odds *were* in their favor. We found confirmation of this belief from most of our subjects, who believed that their chances of being caught were, on the whole, very slim. For example, in response to a question about how many times they thought they could smuggle drugs into the United States without getting caught, responses included these.

> If it hadn't been for a snitch, I could have done it indefinitely. The money overrode any—any rational judgment. (12)

> My percentage all the time, 99 percent [chance of getting away with it], and it always worked out 99 percent because if it was done right . . . (6)

Unless there is an informant involved your odds are 95 percent in your favor. Zero, zero [chance of getting caught]. I've had some trying times when I figured in danger, but not by the police. Usually it was the elements. (24)

I can tell you, you can do it all the times you want, and we cannot get caught. Well if we break down, okay, if we get unlucky, like there happens to be a cop right there when you're coming in you know, those chances you always got that. (32)

Role of Conviction

Most individuals we spoke to rated the chances of arrest as very slim. They saw their chances of conviction as even slimmer. However, that belief was countered by their experiences, where, it seemed to them, everyone was convicted in the federal system. As one individual put it, "arrest equals imprisonment."

I didn't—I had no idea how the—the legal system worked. I was totally unaware of how it was stacked, and it's stacked pretty steeply in their favor. Even if you have—even if their case is weak, they can get you convicted. They could convict a dead cat, I think. (12)

[Question: What did you think your chances of being convicted were?] Slim and none. (6)

They told me one day, Hey the law is ten to life. So what? I didn't know. I didn't know that five people could stand in court and lie against me and get me convicted because with the trip that I got convicted twenty-seven years, I had nothing to do with that trip. (32)

[Question: So if you are arrested, you're almost always convicted?] Yeah. (21)

Role of Imprisonment

Just as was the case with prosecution and conviction, most subjects had no idea about the likely penalties for drug smuggling. This was not surprising, as few citizens are knowledgeable about sentencing guidelines. There was also little knowledge of the conspiracy charge and the elements necessary to prove such a charge. This was reflected in smugglers' decisions to take the risks they took. They saw little chance of arrest or conviction, and they figured that sentences would be finite and relatively short, on average about ten years. Once in prison, enlightened by experience, their views changed sharply.

> I thought maybe ten years, I always accepted ten years. Maybe if I would have had something concrete that I knew I was going to get that time, I would have stopped. (22)

> I didn't know they didn't have it [parole]. I could handle ten years without parole. I couldn't handle any more. (5)

> Of course you do [think about the sentence]. But when you're making money, your mind sometimes—you think you're indestructible. (8)

> Ten years you begin to say, whoa, if I get caught I lose ten years of my life. I don't know. (7)

> I never thought they were going to give me life. (3)

Role of Getting Caught

We observed three key outcomes when we asked subjects about the effect of getting caught. The first question was whether being caught and imprisoned was likely to make someone stop smuggling drugs in the future. By and large, subjects told us that their imprisonment, for whatever reason, was likely to cause them to quit smuggling drugs. The second issue was increased knowledge of the criminal justice system. As noted above, not one subject was aware of the length of the sentence awaiting him at the conclusion of his trial. The third issue was the smugglers' age on release. Most received sentences long enough that they would be old men on release or they would be buried at the prison. These three factors combined to lead all but one subject to tell us that their smuggling days were over.

> [I] would never do it again. Being here you learn a lot by talking to other drug smugglers. I would never do it over. (34)

> There is always the risk, but the risk—if I'm going to say I'm going to make three million dollars and I'm broke—right now, if you ask me would I do it again I would tell you no because—not because of the time that I got or—because of what, you know the suffering of my family, my sons, my daughter, you know. (31)

> The first thing I am going to do [when I get out] is try and see if I can find a job that doesn't—doesn't put me back into what I did. I would never even think about it. I don't care honestly—if I got to live underneath a bridge, never. (22)

> I would not get involved in narcotics again because all I got from that is pain, you know. Yes, one can make a lot of money, a lot of money, but is not worth it. (9)

A single subject offered an imaginary scenario about resuming his former career.

> So an imaginary person. This imaginary person will probably go to it again because you got to figure this. This person—the system does not work. He's not a shoemaker. He's not a doctor. He doesn't know how to build houses, but yet he knows how to smuggle and he's very good in the logistics

and he's very good with people. So chances are he's going back to it. (29)

Role of Conspiracy

Above we noted the role of conspiracy in convicting drug smugglers. A conspiracy charge does not require an individual to have committed an overt act. Being captured on tape discussing a drug smuggling opportunity is often sufficient for conviction on conspiracy to import or distribute drugs. In such cases, individuals were surprised to find themselves charged with sentences of thirty years or, in some cases, life imprisonment.

A second element of the process of catching drug smugglers bears noting in this context. Most individuals we interviewed were not caught with drugs in their possession. Being caught with drugs or in a conspiracy where there are actually drugs is known as a wet conspiracy. In dry conspiracies, no drugs are ever involved, and smugglers are convicted for discussing, arranging, or organizing drug smuggling operations with agents of the U.S. government even though no drugs were ever transported or touched as part of the conspiracy. This is, to observe the obvious, a very powerful tool for law enforcement. Not surprisingly, the individuals we interviewed who were convicted in dry conspiracies did not know of this tactic and resented it. Most saw it as inconsistent with the U.S. Constitution.

[Question: What did you think your chances of being convicted were?] Like I said, as far as myself and the general public is concerned you get caught with your hands in the cookie jar, you did it. I never had it around me or anything like that. I had no idea that the government operated the way they operate. They said I was being arrested on a violation of narcotics. I said, "Narcotics? I don't have anything on me." They looked at me and laughed and said, "You don't need to." If I knew about conspiracy I would have been out [of the drug smuggling business] like a bat out of hell. (6)

Since this conspiracy where they throw my name in here was a cocaine conspiracy. Then I was put and accused of conspiracy to import cocaine. It was a dry conspiracy. But there is no doubt that this conspiracy did exist. [Just not the drugs.] (28)

Just say, "How about a drug deal" with your friend. You know, that's enough to convict you with a life sentence, just by knowing the drug dealer and saying that's your friend. That's enough to convict you with a life sentence because anything that drug dealer is involved in, because of the conspiracy laws, you are involved in it. It was drugs involved, but I never saw the drugs. (19)

[Question: Do you think people out there understand the conspiracy law?] No, no. They have to feel it. They have to feel it to know what it is. I never think I'd be convicted. If it doesn't the conspiracy law, I wouldn't be here. (33)

If You Were in Charge

Near the conclusion of each interview, we asked the subject a question that usually surprised him. We turned the tables on this group of drug smugglers and asked them for their recommendations about dealing with the drug problem in the United States. We asked for their policy recommendations, the steps they would take, if they were in charge of drug policy in this country. Their recommendations fell into four categories.

The first category of recommendations argued that legalization was the only way to effectively deal with the problem. This group of respondents argued that unless the profit was taken out of drugs, there would be no stopping the importation of or the demand for drugs.

Take the profit out of it. Put drugs in a drugstore. Decriminalize it, legalize it. Everybody has got a price and I suppose even the pope does, you know. (12)

The second recommendation was to reduce demand. This involved either the introduction of rehabilitation programs for current users or education for school-age children.

Spend more money on the demand, the people that use the drugs. Take care of the users. (34)

I don't want to say this but I think that the American people are—is a society who is overmedicated who is always looking for drugs, something to be high all the time. (26)

Understand that the only way is by trying to cut the demand. If there is no demand there is no buying. If there is consumption there will be demand. (30)

If you wanted to reduce it—and this is not going to happen overnight—it's you've got to reduce the demand. That's the only thing. (24)

So the problem is not cocaine, the problem is not heroin or crack, the problem is the education of the American youth and the American people not to do the drugs, which it is proven that can be done. (13)

The third set of recommendations were to change law enforcement tactics and to increase publicity about conspiracy laws.

Blockade the source countries. (28)

You can educate the government to think the way that the smugglers would think, and that would stop a lot of flow. (32)

They [Customs and Coast Guard] need to work harder, search longer and harder when they stop a boat. Use a naval architect. (25)

Conspiracy is the key to stopping any drug operation, any kind of illegal activity because conspiracy is you don't need drugs in order to be convicted for it. (19)

The final group was a mixture of interventions on a more global scale.

They purchase cheese and give it to poor people in this country. They could do the same thing [for poor people in Colombia]. They don't want to do it. (31)

Summary

The information presented in this chapter confirms that U.S. enforcement efforts have required smugglers to take precautions to minimize perceived risks and avoid detection. The result has been increasing sophistication of their operations, which increases the number of people involved and therefore the risks to those managing the operations. Unfortunately for law enforcement, these risks were overlooked by smugglers in light of technological advances that have helped foster a sense of immunity among transporters—a sense that was strengthened by each successful smuggling venture. It was clear that the smugglers did not consider smuggling drugs into the United States to have been a risky career because they did not perceive a high level of threat from U.S. law enforcement and the criminal justice system.

However, this assessment was based on misconceptions that they could spend time in prison only if they were caught with drugs and that their time in prison would be brief should they be sentenced. Had they conceived of the possibility of serving a sentence for conspiring to traffic drugs, they may have changed their practices. Those who reconsidered their actions in light of their experiences with the U.S. criminal justice system expressed frustration with the "new tools" (i.e., the use of confidential informants and cooperating defendants to convict on conspiracy charges), and they showed an increased reluctance to traffic drugs again in light of the significant sentences attached to the charges they considered "bogus." This is an important finding for law enforcement, encouraging the continued use of the valuable tools of confidential informants and snitches to reach beyond the network. In addition to debunking the myth that smugglers can be arrested only if they are caught with drugs, the government should also broadly advertise the potential sentence for someone convicted of conspiring to traffic or caught while trafficking drugs into the United States.

7 Making Sense of Drug Smuggling

Conclusions and Summary

Studies of crime and deviance typically begin with the question, "Why do people commit crime?" However, in the case of international drug smuggling, it may be more appropriate to ask why people do not smuggle drugs. Hirschi (1969) and Gottfredson and Hirschi (1979) point out that conformity, not deviance, should be questioned. Such a view of the motivation for engaging in international drug smuggling should receive special focus, given the perception that enormous profits can be made, the difficulties facing law enforcement in catching smugglers, and the relatively low levels of skill needed to work in a drug smuggling group. As we have seen, the motivation to become involved in illegal drug smuggling is generated with considerable ease. Three other considerations are important in this context: the seemingly unlimited profits to be made, the apparent ease of successfully smuggling drugs, and the widespread availability of drugs in the United States.

It is against this backdrop that we conclude this insider's view into the world of international drug smuggling. We focus on three topics: the organizational structure of drug smuggling, the management of risk by those involved in such enterprises, and the potential response by law enforcement.

Organizational Structure

We interviewed 34 drug smugglers, reviewed the case files of 297 drug smugglers, interviewed federal agents, and reviewed dozens of official documents and studies of international drug smuggling. These analyses produce a view of the organizational structure of international drug smuggling that is at variance with the public and at times law enforcement perceptions about the structure of such enterprises. Our research led us to the conclusion that drug smuggling efforts are not well organized other than at the points that large sums of money are exchanged, that they often involve low-level offenders recruited for temporary roles, and that they involve little specialization.

Rather than being hierarchical, rigidly controlled cartels, the drug smuggling organizations described by the individuals we interviewed were more like the small cells or networks described by Williams (1998: 155) as "a series of connected nodes." These versatile organizational forms are made effective by their dynamic and flexible nature. Most importantly, the networks facilitate the flow of information through a structure that includes both a core and several peripheries. The peripheries are the network's most vulnerable locus; they are where the network is most exposed to public view, particularly to law enforcement surveillance activities. Individuals involved in the periphery of criminal networks are tied to each other by their current—and prior—involvement in criminal activities.

Best and Luckenbill (1994: 5) developed a typology based on the association of individuals involved in transactions to describe the social organization of deviance. They argued that most deviance is not particularly well organized, though their primary focus was on deviance rather than on such serious felonies as drug smuggling. In general, these researchers described associations among offenders that are not especially formal, that have short lives, and that are organized around specific transactions. The salient characteristics of the organization are found not in the structure of the group but rather in the nature of the interactions and transactions in which its members engage. The key to understanding the way such events are organized is the nature of the interaction before, during, and after the transaction. This is particularly relevant to the social organization of drug smuggling as described by our subjects.

Donald and Wilson (2000) reiterate a common theme in the study of the organizational structure of offending groups: that offenders do not organize themselves very effectively. This conclusion spans burglars (Shover, 1996; Wright and Decker, 1994), robbers (Einstadter, 1969; Wright and Decker, 1997), carjackers (Jacobs, Topali, and Wright, 2003), and gang members (Decker, Bynum, and Weisel, 1998; Klein, 1995). To better understand these groups of offenders, Donald and Wilson (2000) contrast teams and coacting. In the case of teams, there is considerable interdependence among actors, with the net result that team action is a whole that is greater than the sum of its parts. Coacting, on the other hand, produces little interdependence among actors; consequently, congregate behavior among such relationships rarely produces little of additional value that accrues to the efforts of the group. In their study of ram raiding—smash, force entry, grab, and flee—Donald and Wilson found a preponderance of evidence to support their view that such offenders are versatile and show little evidence of specialization. Offenders have "connections" (Shover, 1996; Decker and Van Winkle, 1996) that enable them to assemble crews, identify targets, dispose of goods, learn about risks of detection, and seek safety. But such linkages are the product of generalized offending roles, weak ties, and fluid relationships. On a continuum between co-offending groups (individuals who offend together without role distinctions or specializations) and teams (more distinct roles, some evidence of specialization, and at least a moderate amount of cohesion among affiliates), these low-level street offenders most closely correspond to the category of co-offenders. Similarly,

Schiray (2001) notes that specialization can be episodic in the international drug trade and that smugglers can be absorbed into other forms of criminality. He notes that specialization is particularly likely to occur in the area of money laundering, where it is often linked to businesses operating on the periphery of legality. Our conclusion is that the organization of international drug smugglers more closely resembles that of street offenders than it does a corporate structure.

The social organization of international drug smuggling has been studied in the Dutch context by Zaitch (2002), who conducted extensive fieldwork in Colombia and the Netherlands to better understand the movement of cocaine from Colombia to Europe, specifically to the Netherlands. Zaitch found that although Colombians were integrally involved in the movement of cocaine to the Netherlands, there was little evidence of vertical hierarchies in drug smuggling; the structure of drug distribution was more flexible than rigid, more horizontal than vertical, and kinship and ethnicity played important roles in generating trust, particularly among Colombians. The kinship ties did not make Colombian drug smuggling a family business, but instead facilitated transactions based on affective relations. Similar to our own findings, Zaitch found that ethnicity and language also helped facilitate relations among smugglers, though he described an enterprise remarkably easy for Colombians to penetrate. He described drug smuggling operations as flexible networks (240), a conclusion that underscores the need for dynamic, insulated, transaction groups capable of quickly changing their tactics while remaining relatively isolated from successive steps in the chain of smuggling.

In his observations of drug smuggling in Sao Paulo, Brazil, Schiray (2001) described the organizational structure of drug distribution markets as "ad hoc organizations" that are "precarious, provisional, short-lived and contingent" (355), in stark contrast to the formal corporate structures so often used to describe such organizations. He noted that they lacked stability and were short-lived, making them adaptable to changing internal and external conditions and in turn more difficult to counter with traditional suppression techniques.

International trafficking in stolen vehicles provides an interesting contrast to international drug smuggling. Clarke and Brown (2003) found that the process of such trafficking is comprised of a series of interrelated steps, but that the links between the steps are not necessarily well organized or orchestrated. These researchers concluded that such processes are generally not well organized and often are disconnected. This bears a strong resemblance to the depiction of drug smuggling organizations we have presented here. Although drug smuggling to the Netherlands and Brazil and auto theft in an international context differ in countries involved and offense type, the findings are consistent with our conclusions regarding the nature of drug smuggling organizations, and they lend support to this view of the structure of such offending.

Drug smugglers are typically involved in other crimes. The most obvious form of criminality is drug use, but there are others. Any pockets of specialization typically prove to be short-lived as offenders drift to more generalized involvement in crime (Schiray, 2003: 5). Specialization within organizations typically requires a structure to integrate it with other organizational functions. Most drug smuggling lacks the requisite level of organizational structure to support a high degree of specialization or specialization that occurs for a prolonged period of time. Many drug smugglers make their way into smuggling roles through contacts with other offenders that expand their "criminal capital"—their knowledge of and familiarity with other offenders who can ease them into new forms of criminality. Similarly, specialists can evolve into generalists as a consequence of their contact with generalists involved in smuggling enterprises. This suggests that there is a general pattern of offending that links involvement in drug smuggling to involvement in other offenses, which reinforces the value of explanations that emphasize general patterns of offending as well as more comprehensive theories of crime, rather than those that emphasize specialization.

Our data fail to provide support for offending specialization. The lack of specialization diminishes the probability that smugglers are part of a more sophisticated organization, since specialization is a key aspect of organizational differentiation and sophistication. Without a structure to generate and support it, specialization rarely emerges among co-offenders or members of loosely coupled groups. Schiray (2003: 5) characterizes Brazilian drug smuggling groups as having "horizontal" organizational structures that lack formal roles, group structure, stable leadership, and permanence. Such groups may have sporadic relationships with tightly coupled organizations that have vertical structures, but the relationships are task-specific and rarely change the nature of the horizontal groups.[1]

The transition from the Medellin to Cali cartels and then to small networks illustrates that both internal and external forces produce change in the structure of drug distribution. But most importantly, such structures are dynamic, and they change as a means of survival, often assuming forms that contradict the structure of their predecessors. A hostile external environment often produces adaptation and change that makes an organization more effective (Hedberg, 1981). Bunker and Sullivan (1998: 58) observed three distinct phases in the evolution of the organizational structure of drug distribution in the Caribbean. They identified the aggressive Medellin model as the first phase, followed by the Cali model that co-opted its enemies and then by the more loosely coupled third-phase organizations that rely heavily on technology. Williams (1998: 157) observed that the vertically integrated distribution model of the Medellin and Cali cartels transformed into a network-based model because of the virtues for trafficking that the diversity of such networks provided. Such virtues include the ability to manage large numbers of disparate groups, to maintain distance between the groups, and to respond in a dynamic and rapid fashion to challenges presented by enforcement, market conditions, and the environment in the Caribbean. Another virtue of such networks is the extent to which they serve to insulate important stages of the distribution process from each other. This is particularly the case for the brokers and owners of the loads of drugs in Colombia, who may never leave their own country, are not known to those at other stages of the distribution process, and as such are insulated from detection in the Caribbean and the United States. Individuals in Colombia are further insulated from other stages of the distribution process by language and ethnicity, a recurrent theme expressed in our interviews. Perhaps the most important part of the drug smuggling process is the receipt of the money for the load and its transfer to the office in Colombia. Not surprisingly, this is the most organized and highly compartmentalized aspect of the entire transaction.

Managing Risk

Like most offenders, drug smugglers search for a way to believe that they will not get caught. We refer to this process as risk management. Smugglers try to find a comfort zone in which they believe that the odds of getting away with the crime are in their favor. After all, they could not and would not smuggle if they did not think this way. In this manner, they are like most other offenders—particularly property offenders—who also convince themselves that the odds of getting away with the crime are in their favor. They achieve this state by engaging in a series of behaviors that they believe reduce their risks of being detected or, if detected, of being held legally liable. Such a comfort zone is the product of a "calculus" that identifies known risks, creates a series of steps to reduce those known risks, and tests the likely effectiveness of such steps.

As Williams (1998) notes, networks have a number of self-protective mechanisms, not the least of which are their lack of formal structures, permanence, and redundancy. In our case, ethnicity and language also play important roles in helping insulate drug smuggling networks from penetration by law enforcement because of the heightened importance of culture, especially Caribbean seagoing culture among the traffickers and Colombian culture among the owners and brokers. Perrow's (1999) distinction between tightly and loosely coupled organizations is critical here. Tightly coupled organizations manifest vulnerabilities to outside disturbances or interference that are not found in loosely coupled networks, where linkages are far less formal and less well understood by participants. As such, loosely coupled networks of drug smugglers are less vulnerable to outside penetration and are much more capable of regenerating themselves if they are penetrated, disrupted, or dismantled. In the view of tightly coupled formal organizations, their loosely coupled counterparts are inefficient because of their redundant, weakly tied, and less-structured character. However, in the case of international drug smuggling, it is precisely those characteristics that make loosely coupled groups a superior mechanism for transporting drugs internationally.

One of the missing considerations in much of the deterrence or risk reduction literature is the magnitude of potential gain. In the case of drug smuggling, the magnitude of gain can be immense. Indeed, part of the calculus for drug smugglers is to conceptualize the gain as immense, even if it does not turn out to be large. Hedberg (1981) refers to this belief as a myth told by members of organizations to convince others—and often themselves—of the prospects of reward. As we learned from many of our subjects, the actual gain often falls far short of the hypothesized gain. But the myth of large gain serves to keep members of a network together and encourages them to assume larger risks than they otherwise might.

Risk management is a key to continued participation in drug smuggling. Zabludoff (1997: 30–31) identified seven key tactics by which risk can be reduced within networked groups:

1. Changing methods quickly and often
2. Outsourcing wherever possible
3. Getting collateral from others in the distribution chain
4. Providing payments in product rather than cash
5. Dividing the operation into compartmentalized functions

6. Limiting the amount of time that the product and money are in transit
7. Clearly identifying who pays for lost product

These lessons clearly were not studied in a school context by our subjects, but they were reflected in practice. The international drug smugglers whose networks we came to understand learned these principles through trial and error. In particular, the outsourcing of functions such as making loads of drugs, transporting the drugs, and retailing them were staples of the operations described by our subjects. Such operations were closely linked to the compartmentalization of smuggling such that individuals from one function never knew or were aware of those from another function. Such a general approach to risk reduction and management is clearly more effectively carried out within an organizational structure with limited spheres of contact between the levels, and one that is highly compartmentalized with limited movement of information between levels. The fragmentation of this process works to insulate those in Colombia from the levels of transactions that could put them at heightened risk of identification and detection.

The key component in the calculus is to know the risks. That is, it is imperative to learn what risks exist and their likelihood of occurring, and then to devise strategies to manage those risks. This is a key to understanding how international drug smuggling is organized. Such an understanding will have direct utility in disrupting drug smuggling. Introducing unknown risks or disorder into the process of smuggling can be powerfully disruptive beyond the specific individual deterrence that is produced. Uncertainty makes owners less likely to seek brokers, makes brokers more reluctant to put loads together, makes it harder to recruit captains, and makes it harder for captains to recruit crews, transshipment teams, and offloaders at the arrival ports. Such market uncertainty can come from using snitches or undercover agents, making changes in enforcement and surveillance techniques, and using conspiracy charges (whether wet or dry). In the end, market uncertainty is the key to disrupting active distribution chains. Disorder disrupts smugglers' confidence and produces a loss of trust; in the absence of a structured organization with formal rules and channels of communication, trust is key to the way the drug smuggling operation functions. The absence of a structure that can overcome or counter disruptions to the market appears to be a point of vulnerability for less structured organizations.

Potential Responses by Law Enforcement

A key challenge to law enforcement is the high profitability of cocaine smuggling. However, the profits are not evenly distributed across the roles involved in growth, production, shipping, and wholesaling the drug. As MacCoun and Reuter (2001) found for street-level crack distribution, the profits from such sales are often relatively small compared to the large sums of money made in wholesaling the drug. Zabludoff (1997) and Schiray (2001) made similar observations about the roles involved in international cocaine distribution; those involved in putting together loads or arranging for shipping in Colombia stand to make large profits, but the people at either earlier or later stages of the distribution chain may not fare as well. In addition, many of those at the later end of the distribution chain may be paid in product, exposing them to further risk of apprehension as well as discounting their gain. It is important to recall that a great deal of the profit margin in the production and distribution of cocaine is a result of the illegality of the drug. Much is produced and lost, reflecting the volume of raw product that is produced and the very high profits associated with the drugs that make it from the source country to the consumption country.

Law enforcement faces other challenges in generating an effective response to drug smuggling. It is worth asking the question: at which points does disorder affect the production and distribution chains of narcotics, and how does the disorder affect the people at those points? The growth of coca plants seems to involve little risk of exposure to arrest or prosecution. The risk increases at the harvesting and processing of the crop, but it remains lower than at other stages in the production and distribution of the drug. These observations are particularly true of the role that U.S. enforcement plays in disrupting drug markets. Because these two steps occur outside the sovereignty of the U.S. government, they are more difficult to penetrate and disrupt. Once the plants are grown and processed, loads must be put together for transport. This is a significant stage at which money and product must be exchanged, producing some vulnerabilities. Again, because these steps generally occur beyond the reach of the U.S. government, they are less vulnerable to enforcement efforts without the assistance of a willing and able partner.

When the product leaves the source country (Colombia in our study), it becomes vulnerable to increased surveillance and suppression efforts, though our work has documented the difficulties faced by enforcement efforts. The arrival of the drug into the United States is another point of high vulnerability for disrupting and interdicting the drug. However, once the drug has been moved from wholesale to retail distribution levels, the task for law enforcement becomes more difficult because the distribution agents, while more visible, are lower level, more plentiful, and more easily replaced if arrested or taken out of the supply chain. Zabludoff (1997: 34) argues that the distribution chain is most vulnerable where money is exchanged, and it is there, consequently, where law enforcement efforts to suppress and disrupt drug distribution must be focused.

Poor countries, whose sovereignty is often destabilized by a strong drug economy, may have economic dependence on the production and marketing of the drug, may be unable to effectively counter the organization of drug production, or both. In addition, because the initial stages of growth, production, and preparation for shipping of cocaine occur outside the sovereignty of the United States, partnerships are critical for effective enforcement. For these reasons as well as because of inadequate or corrupt law enforcement in the source country, such cooperation is either difficult to obtain or comes at a high price. But even when cooperation is forthcoming, the high demand for cocaine in the United States effectively thwarts or subverts suppression efforts. Indeed, one of our subjects told us that if demand was not so high in the United States, he would ship the cocaine elsewhere. This subject wryly observed that he did not see a need to look for alternative markets. It is important to note that some smugglers have high levels of sophistication and can effectively thwart suppression efforts. While all the subjects we interviewed had been caught and prosecuted, many of them had eluded capture for years and had smuggled tons of cocaine into the United States.

There is an important caveat to this view of market suppression and disruption: the combination of the sheer volume of cocaine available for shipment and the demand for the drug in the United States. Given these factors, it is worth considering the consequences of launching 1 million rafts, each with a ton of cocaine, off the coast of Colombia, targeted to drift toward South Florida or other U.S. destinations. This "bulk" model, in which a small fraction of the product is expected to make it to market in the United States, carries little risk of detection for individuals and is still consistent with an attempt to meet demand. Compare that to a submarine with a small load of drugs but high probability of getting through.[2] As long as enough product gets through and the money comes back to the offices in Colombia, a transaction is successful from the perspective of those who produce and control the drug in Colombia.

This mental exercise raises the question about the stage in the process of producing and distributing the drug at which it assumes its monetary value. The closer the drug gets to the street, the higher its monetary value. Thus the largest cost component of the drug is not its growth or production, but rather transportation and wholesale distribution in the destination country. As long as enough product gets to the street to generate profit, the money lost and the number of arrests do not matter to those in Colombia because of the large volume of the drug available. This underscores a key difference between the people in Colombia and those in transportation roles. In Colombia, as long as enough drug goes through, that is fine. From the transporter to the end distribution point, as long as their load goes through, their goals have been met. This underscores the divergent goals of people across the networks—goals so divergent that it is difficult to include them as a part of the same organization.

Changing the dominant view of the organizational structure, as well as the institutional legacy of the way that the U.S. law enforcement community views drug smuggling, is a major challenge. Fixed images of a problem are not germane only to the understanding of international drug smuggling among law enforcement personnel. Intelligence-based enforcement and suppression efforts are based on long-term studies, gathering of evidence, undercover work, and assembling the data to form a meaningful picture of offending. The images of offending patterns and organization are not built quickly; they require considerable triangulation of data and method and a high level of skill to effectively create policy and responses. Because of the work that goes into creating intelligence-based views of drug smuggling (and other forms of offending), the views are not easily dismissed or changed, often to the detriment of enforcement efforts. Our research has amply documented the extent to which individuals involved in drug smuggling work in dynamic, often precarious settings that demand rapid change. A key challenge for law enforcement is to avoid a fixed image of the problem, as the problem assuredly changes routinely. Naylor (1997) has been critical of the application of traditional categories of economic activity by law enforcement in understanding drug transactions, arguing that such categories are misleading and create a mistaken understanding of the nature of relationships among the stages and actors in drug smuggling.

The problem of a fixed image of the problem is not confined to views of international drug smuggling; it is true in the criminal justice response to gangs (Katz and Webb, 2006; McCorkle and Meithe, 2001), international terrorism (Rosenfeld, 2004), and drug enforcement (Weisburd and Braga, 2006). Enforcement groups develop an institutional framework for typifying and responding to issues, and in a sense agencies and officials become trapped by their own views. When markets or offenders are dynamic or when offenders fail to conform to the dominant view, the official responses are geared to deal with problems that in a real sense no longer exist. Indeed, the key challenges to law enforcement in responding to terrorism, cyber-crime, international drug smuggling, and human trafficking, among others, are to understand the movement, structure and change in information associated with these activities (Burt, 1992; Arquilla and Ronfeldt, 1997).

The U.S. drug smuggling response conceptualizes drug markets in a particular manner. Federal law enforcement and prosecution in the United States go after organizations (typically conceptualized as RICO prosecutions), not after networks, and therefore may miss important ways of conceptualizing drug smuggling. The organizational structure is the key. Effective policy and responses to drug smuggling require understanding the way smuggling is organized, or at least appreciating its diversity. Too often, policy and responses focus on the visible and most easily controlled aspects of international drug smuggling, the people at the end of the distribution chain who are most visible, yet least knowledgeable about the most important steps in the process.

The premise of drug smuggling is that it is highly organized, pays high dividends, has high rewards, is easily to recruit for and involves a large area for law enforcement to surveil. The reality is different and presents many challenges to law enforcement. These include the use of small cells that are not interconnected, the lack of connection to institutions in the United States, the lack of specialization, the use of multiple pathways to smuggle the drug into the United States, the dynamic nature of the organizations, and the self-contained nature of most of the networks.

Zabludoff (1997) observes the following key challenges:

1. The real bosses are in Colombia, where they are insulated, perhaps even protected, from U.S. law enforcement.
2. Fragmentation makes law enforcement more difficult. The large number of small targets is harder to address than a smaller number of large targets would be.
3. There is considerable flexibility, adaptation, and ability to learn and adapt quickly to changes in law enforcement tactics.

It is against this backdrop that we offer several recommendations for responding to international drug smuggling in the United States. These recommendations are consistent with our findings, particularly the findings about the nature of organization within drug smuggling chains. The United States should continue to use confidential informants and conspiracy charges to interrupt the managed risk principle under which most offenders work. However, such tactics are successful only if smugglers believe that there is a real chance that they will fall subject to them. Deterrence works only when individuals are aware of the risks and believe that they could actually be caught and convicted. Most of the offenders we interviewed did not know what a dry conspiracy was, but they were quick to point out its strong deterrent value. There is also a strong deterrent value in long sentences. Most of our subjects were unable to accurately estimate the amount of prison time they were subject to prior to being caught, and they were unpleasantly surprised by the length of their sentences. In this regard, we recommend more widely publicizing the sentencing guidelines where publicity will do the most good—where they will come to the attention of those involved in, at the periphery of, or likely to become involved in international drug smuggling. Publicizing the length of prison sentences, the use of dry conspiracies, and the elderly age at which most smugglers will be released from custody in U.S. prisons must be done through popular culture outlets in Caribbean and South American contexts.

We also recommend that law enforcement challenge itself to avoid the use of fixed images of problems. This is particularly true of crimes that involve an international context, such as international drug smuggling, human trafficking, identity theft, terrorism, and the movement of stolen goods. Law enforcement is not unlike most other institutions and agencies that become trapped by old business models or fixed images of dynamic problems or that resort to common sets of institutional practices. Life in the information age is driven by new realities; those who are slow to grasp the realities will be losers. The winners may not be governments but instead the small, self-contained networks of motivated individuals focused on a single goal for a short period of time. In many instances, the network may have achieved its goal and vanished before it can be detected.

Building strong governments in countries that are potential sources of drug production seems an obvious suggestion. Many countries with large narco-economies have a difficult time dealing with the challenges presented by these illegal economies and the violence and corruption they create. That said, until demand for illegal drugs can be curtailed in the United States, such efforts are not likely to pay large dividends.

It is always important to consider the latent consequences of a successful enforcement policy. One latent consequence may be displacement of illegal drugs to alternative source countries or transshipment locations. There is evidence of displacement to Europe (Zaitch, 2002) and Mexico (DEA, 1997). In addition, a shift in drug type, as well as in the production modality for the drugs, may occur. There is emerging evidence that methamphetamine increasingly is being produced in Mexico and smuggled into the United States. According to the United Nations, international cocaine seizures set a record in 2004, increasing 18 percent to 588 metric tons (2005: 87). The UN also noted that Colombia is now the site of the largest volume of seizures, reflecting a change from the time our interviews were conducted, and that Mexico has become the primary transshipment site. These changes underscore the primary findings of our research: drug smuggling organizations are highly flexible and dynamic and respond to external pressures.

In conclusion, the challenges to interdiction of illegal drugs are many. If easy responses to interdiction exist, they would have been found and implemented. Among the greatest challenges is the sheer size of the Caribbean, a body of water roughly the size of the continental United States. In addition, there was a widely held lottery mentality among our subjects; they believed that they were going to hit it big on the next shipment. The lure of huge profits (whether false or true) was sufficient to motivate many subjects to take foolish risks. As we reviewed the evidence from our interviews, we heard a common refrain: almost with disdain for Americans, they told us that they wouldn't ship cocaine to the United States if there wasn't such high demand. Addressing that demand may be the most salient and difficult way to effectively address international drug smuggling.

Appendix 1

Instrumentation Study Design

ID # _____

Drug Smuggling Questionnaire for Interviews

Hi. My name is _____.
[Read informed consent.] **I understand that you are in prison as a result of a drug trafficking charge. This study seeks to understand how people become involved in drug trafficking.**

    I. **First, I would like to begin by asking you a few questions about your background and contact with the criminal justice system.** *[Answer all questions in this section.]*

       1. Age _____

       2. In what country were you born? _____

          Citizenship _____

          Ethnicity _____

       3. Education

          Highest Grade Completed _____

4. Prior Criminal Justice Contact with U.S. Law Enforcement Officials

   Age at First Arrest _____

   Offense at First Arrest _____

   Number of Prior Arrests _____

   Age at First Conviction _____

   Offense at First Conviction _____

5. Prior criminal justice contact with non–U.S. law enforcement officials

   Age at first arrest _____

   Offense at first arrest _____

   Number of Prior Arrests _____

   Age at First Conviction _____

   Offense at First Conviction _____

6. Age at First Drug Smuggling Arrest _____

   Offense at First Drug Smuggling Arrest _____

   Number of Drug Smuggling Arrests _____

   Country of Residence at First Drug Smuggling Arrest _____

   Location of First Drug Smuggling Arrest _____

   Age at First Drug Smuggling Conviction _____

   Offense at First Drug Smuggling Conviction _____

   Number of Drug Smuggling Convictions _____

   Country of Residence at First Drug Smuggling Conviction _____

   Location of First Drug Smuggling Conviction _____

[10 MINUTES]

II. Now, I would like you to describe the drug smuggling offense that resulted in your incarceration, in general terms. *[Answer all questions with underlines.]*

7. <u>Current Offense</u>

   Date of Arrest _____

   Charge at Arrest _____

   Date of Conviction _____

   Sentence Length _____

   Conviction Offense _____

8. What <u>type of drugs</u> were you smuggling? _____

   What was the <u>size</u> of the load (kilos)? _____

   How was the load packaged? _____

   What was its estimated <u>value in the United States</u>? _____

   Did you pay for it? _____

   If so, how much? _____

   Where did the load <u>originate</u>? _____

   What was the <u>final destination</u> point? _____

   What were the <u>routes and types of conveyances</u> that were going to be used to get the drugs to the final destination point? (locations of pick-up points, trans-shipment points, stash points, delivery points, POE) _____

   Who was the <u>original owner</u> of the load? (Specify whether an organization and/or single or multiple owners) _____

   Did <u>ownership</u> of the load <u>change</u> at different points in the smuggling operation? _____ If so, when? _____

   What <u>part of the smuggling operation did you participate in</u>? (Specify shipment points and method) _____

   Therefore, which of the following would you say best describes your <u>role in the offense</u> for which you are currently serving federal time?

Smuggler   Source   Financier

Pilot   Air Crew   Boat Captain   Sea Crew

Lookout   offloader   longshoreman

Courier   (Specify Route)   Air   Sea   Land

Other (Specify) _____

Lawyer   CJS (employee) _____

      A. How <u>were you recruited</u> for this role? _____

What <u>payment and instructions</u> were provided to you? _____

What were you told would *happen* if the <u>load were stolen/lost/interdicted</u>? _____

What was the nationality of the driver/boat captain/pilot? _____

Was s/he trained to counter law enforcement entities? _____

Were the drugs <u>hidden in a compartment</u> specifically manufactured for drug smuggling or were you using an existing void or space? _____

If modified, how? _____

By what type of person? _____   Where? _____

And how were the drugs going to be accessed from the compartment? _____

What was the level of confidence that law enforcement would not locate the hidden compartment? _____

Was the conveyance owned by someone or rented? _____

If rented, from what type of company or person? _____

If owned, by what type of person? _____

Did they know it was being used to smuggle drugs? _____

If applicable, did they know it had been modified to smuggle drugs? _____

How many <u>runs were made with this vehicle/boat/plane</u>? _____

What was the make of the vehicle/boat/plane? _____

How many times was it stopped by law enforcement? _____

How did you plan to avoid detection? _____

What techniques did you use to try to avoid detection (spot plane, lookout, and corrupt officials)? _____

Did law enforcement authorities inspect you before departing? _____

Ask the following questions pertaining to the appropriate method. If transportation by air:

Did you have to refuel the plane before reaching your destination? _____

If so, where did you refuel? _____

Did you know the locations of drug enforcement radars? _____

How were you planning to avoid the radars? _____

If transportation by boat:

How was shipment of the load coordinated? (on-load, transit, and off-loads) _____

With what type of person did you communicate with and how often? _____

What was the alternate plan if communication broke down? _____
_____

Did you travel directly to your destination or try to stay close to foreign countries? _____

If so, which ones? _____

Where did you refuel and get your provisions? _____

How much were you going to be paid? _____
($, pesos, contraband)

If contraband, what proportion of the load were you going to get to keep? _____

When were you going to receive your payment? _____

What were you going to do with the money or contraband? _____

Were you surprised when you were caught? _____

Did you think about getting caught? _____

Whose fault was it that you got caught? _____

What did you think your chances of getting caught
were? _____

How did you figure those odds? _____

What did you tell yourself about the risk of being caught that allowed
you to overcome any fears of being caught? _____

[30 MINUTES]

9. **Now I want you to describe your *first* drug smuggling offense
   for me. Use as much detail as you can recall, and remember
   that what you tell me cannot be linked to you.** *[Answer all
   questions with underlines.]*

   How old were you when you first participated in such an
   activity? _____

   What year was it? _____

   How did you come to be involved in drug smuggling? Were you recruited, did you join in with friends, were family members or relatives
   involved in the activity, or did you initiate it on your own? _____

   _____

   Why did you decide to get involved in smuggling drugs? _____

   _____

   How long did you plan on being involved in drug smuggling? _____

   What kind of drug was it? _____

   What was the size of the load (kilos)? _____

   How was the load packaged? _____

   Where did the load originate? _____

What was the final <u>destination</u> point? _____

What <u>routes and types of conveyance</u> were used to get the drugs to the final destination point? (Specify locations for pick-up, transshipment, stash, delivery points, POE) _____

What type of person was the <u>original owner</u> of the load? (Specify whether organization and/or single or multiple owners) _____

Did <u>ownership</u> of the load <u>change</u> at different points in the smuggling operation? _____

What part of the smuggling operation did you <u>participate</u> in? (Specify shipment points and method) _____

Therefore, which of the following would you say best describes your <u>role</u> in your first drug smuggling offense?

Smuggler   Source   Financier

Pilot   Air Crew   Boat Captain   Sea Crew

Lookout   offloader   longshoreman

Courier   (Specify Route)   Air   Sea   Land

Other (Specify) _____

Lawyer   CJS employee (Specify) _____

What <u>payment and instructions</u> were provided to you? _____

What were you told would <u>happen if the load were stolen/lost/ interdicted?</u> _____

What was the nationality of the driver/boat captain/pilot? _____

Was s/he trained to counter law enforcement entities? _____

Were the drugs hidden in a <u>compartment</u> specifically manufactured for drug smuggling or were you using an existing void or space? _____

If modified, how? _____

By what type of person? _____   Where? _____

How were the drugs going to be accessed from the compartment? _____

What was the level of confidence that law enforcement would not locate the hidden compartment? _____

Was the conveyance owned or rented? _____

If rented, from what type of person or company? _____

If owned, by what type of person? _____

Did they know it was being used to smuggle drugs? _____

If applicable, did they know it had been modified to smuggle drugs? _____

What techniques did you use to try to avoid detection (spot planes, lookouts, corrupt officials, etc.)? _____

Did law enforcement authorities inspect you before departing? _____

Ask the following questions pertaining to the appropriate method. If transportation by air:

Did you have to refuel the plane before reaching your destination? _____

If so, where did you refuel? _____

Did you know the locations of drug enforcement radars? _____

How did you plan to avoid them? _____

If transportation by boat:

How was shipment of the load coordinated? (on-load, transit, and off-loads) _____

What type of person did you communicate with and how often? _____

What was the alternate plan if communication broke down? _____

Did you travel directly to your destination or stay close to foreign countries? _____

If so, which ones? _____

Where did you refuel and get your provisions? _____

<u>What</u> were you <u>paid</u>? _____ ($, pesos, contraband)

If contraband, what proportion of the load did you keep? _____

When did you receive it? _____

What did you do with the money or contraband? _____

Did you <u>think</u> about <u>getting caught</u>?   YES   NO

What did you think your <u>chances</u> of getting caught were? _____

How did you <u>figure those</u> odds? _____

What did you tell yourself about the risk of being caught that allowed you to overcome any fears of being caught? _____

Was <u>anyone caught</u> in that drug smuggling activity?   YES   NO

How were they caught? _____

Why were they caught? _____

<u>How did you avoid</u> detection? _____

Why did you continue to smuggle drugs? _____

[45 MINUTES]

10. **Now I want you to think about how many times you have been involved in smuggling drugs into the United States, or as part of a chain that smuggled drugs that ultimately were headed to the United States.** How many times have you been involved in such activities? _____

Have you ever been arrested before?   YES   NO,
IF YES, how many times? _____

Have you ever been convicted before?   YES   NO,
IF YES, how many times?

_____

11. **Now I want you to think about a *typical* drug smuggling activity, the way you usually do it when you smuggled drugs into the United States. Again, we are not interested in information that may be linked to you. *[Answer all questions with underline.]***

How are you typically <u>recruited</u> to participate in an offense? _____

Do you typically <u>work for</u> one individual or organization? _____

How do they usually recruit you? _____

Are they the <u>owners of the load</u>? _____

How does this individual or organization assist you in smuggling drugs into the U.S.? _____

What <u>kind of drug</u> do you typically smuggle into the U.S.? _____

Do you typically carry <u>one type</u> of drug or a variety of drugs? _____

Why? _____

What is the <u>typical size</u> of the load (kilos)? _____

What is the typical <u>method of conveyance</u>? _____

What is the <u>route</u> typically used to smuggle drugs into the U.S.? (Describe where the operation originates from; pick-up, trans-shipment, stash, and drop-off points; and the final destination/ POE) _____

What <u>part</u> of the smuggling operation <u>do you typically participate</u> in? (Specify points and method) _____

Therefore, which of the following would you say best describes your <u>typical role</u> in the offense?
Smuggler   Source   Financier
Pilot   Air Crew   Boat Captain   Sea Crew
Lookout   offloader   longshoreman
Courier   (Specify Route) Air   Sea   Land
Other (Specify) _____

CJS employee (Specify) _____

    B. <u>How many people</u> do you typically work with to transport a load of drugs into the U.S.? _____

What are the <u>roles of the other</u> people you work with to transport a load of drugs into the U.S? _____

Does someone typically provide security? _____

When? _____   Why? _____

Do you typically practice Santeria or voodoo to bless the
load? _____

Have you ever attempted to <u>retaliate or resist law enforcement efforts</u>
with force? _____

In what percentage of trafficking efforts of trafficking events were you
able to use force to resist law enforcement efforts? _____

Do you typically carry a weapon? _____   Why? _____

What is the typical <u>payment and instructions</u> provided
to you? _____

What are you typically told <u>will happen if the load was stolen/lost/
interdicted</u>? _____

What is the typical nationality of the driver/boat captain/pilot? _____

Is s/he typically trained to counter law enforcement entities? _____

How is the load typically <u>packaged</u>? _____

Are the drugs typically hidden in a <u>compartment</u> specifically
manufactured for drug smuggling or were you using an existing
void or space? _____

If modified, how? _____

What type of person typically does this? _____   Where? _____

How are the drugs accessed from the compartment? _____

What is the level of confidence that law enforcement would not locate
the hidden compartment? _____

Is the conveyance typically owned or rented? _____

Do you typically use the <u>same route</u> each time? _____

Is there a <u>certain time of day</u> that you prefer to run the smuggling
operation? _____

If so, when and why? _____

How many <u>runs</u> are typically made <u>with a particular vehicle/boat/plane</u>?

_____

What is the typical make of the vehicle/boat/plane? _____

Is the <u>same driver/pilot/captain</u> used for each event? _____

Why? Why not? _____

How do you typically <u>plan to avoid detection</u>? _____

What <u>techniques</u> did you typically use to try to avoid detection
(spot planes, lookouts, and corrupt officials)? _____

Do law enforcement authorities typically <u>inspect you before
departing</u>? _____

**Ask the following questions pertaining to the appropriate method
identified above.**

If transportation by air:

Do you typically know the <u>locations of drug enforcement radars</u>?

_____

How do you plan to <u>avoid the radars</u>? _____

If transportation by boat:

How is shipment of the load typically coordinated? (on-load, transit,
and off-loads) _____

What type of person do you typically communicate with and how
often? _____

Do you communicate that planes are flying overhead? _____

Is there an alternate plan if communication breaks down? _____

Do you typically take a direct route to your destination or try to stay
close to foreign countries? _____

If so, which ones? _____

What are you typically <u>paid</u>? _____ ($, pesos,
contraband)

If contraband, what proportion of the load do you keep? _____

When do you receive it? _____

What do you do with the money or contraband? _____

Do you think about getting caught?   YES   NO

What do you think your chances of getting caught typically are? _____

How do you figure these odds? _____

What do you tell yourself about the risk of being caught that allows you to continue smuggling drugs? _____

III. Now, I am going to ask you a number of questions related to your assessment of the risks associated with smuggling drugs into the United States. [60 MINUTES. *Answer all of the remaining questions.*]

12. How many times did you think you could smuggle drugs into the US before getting arrested? _____   Convicted? _____

    C. What factors do you use to determine this? (experience, role in offense, luck, mode of transport, etc.) _____

13. On any given attempt, what did you think your chances of being arrested while smuggling drugs into the US is? _____

    D. What do you base this on? _____

    What could increase your risk of being caught? _____

14. On any given attempt, what did you think your chances of being convicted for smuggling drugs into the US is? _____

    E. What do you base this on? _____

15. If you had been convicted of smuggling drugs into the US what sentence did you believe you would receive? _____

16. I want you to think about the chances of being arrested for drug smuggling. If the chances were 1 out of 100, would that stop you from trying to smuggle drugs into the US?   YES   NO.

    What if the chances were 10 out of 100?   YES   NO.

And if the chances were 50 out of 100, would that stop you from trying to smuggle drugs into the US?   YES   NO.

What would your chance of being arrested have to be to make you stop? _____

How many times would you have to be arrested before you would stop trying to smuggle drugs into the US? _____

17. Now I want you to think about the chances of being convicted for smuggling drugs. If the chances were 10 out of 100, would that stop you from trying to smuggle drugs into the US? What about 25 out of 100?   YES   NO.

What about 50 out of 100?   YES   NO.

And finally, what about 90 out of 100? Would that be enough to stop you from smuggling drugs into the US?   YES   NO.

18. Now, let's turn our attention to sentence length. I want you to think about the kind of sentences you might receive for drug smuggling, and whether the threat of such a sentence would be enough to cause you to stop smuggling drugs. If you were arrested and sentenced for drug smuggling, would a sentence of five years be enough to stop you from trying to smuggle drugs into the US?   YES   NO.

What about a sentence of ten years, would that be long enough to cause you to stop trying to smuggle drugs into the US?   YES   NO.

What about a sentence of twenty-five years, would that be long enough to cause you to stop smuggling drugs into the US?   YES   NO.

Finally, what about a life sentence, would that be long enough to cause you to stop smuggling drugs?   YES   NO.

What percentage of your prison sentence do you expect to serve before being released? _____

Did someone in the drug smuggling business tell you that this is what to expect? _____

[90 MINUTES]

19. In general, what is the hardest way to smuggle drugs into the US?

_____

    F. What is the hardest part of the drug smuggling event?

_____

Which of the following roles in drug smuggling has the greatest chance for being caught? The least? Why? _____

How do you get to choose one role over another? _____

Which of the roles is the best? _____

Smuggler   Source   Financier
Pilot   Air Crew   Boat Captain   Sea Crew
Lookout   offloader   longshoreman
Courier   (Route)   Air   Sea   Land
Other (Specify) _____

CJS employee (Specify) _____

Why? _____

Is there a chain of command within smuggling operations? That is, is someone in charge of the entire operation or are they a series of exchanges? _____

20. What is the easiest way (method) to smuggle drugs into the US?

_____

What port of entry is the easiest to smuggle drugs into? _____

The hardest? _____

Why? _____

21. What was your single best score? That is, what drug did you choose, how did you obtain it, how large a load did you get, what was your role, how did it come into the US, and how much money did you make? _____

What is the most important thing to focus on when smuggling drugs into the US? _____

22. I want you to think about the time(s) you were arrested for trying to smuggle drugs into the US. Why were you arrested? _____

    Did you do anything different than you normally do? _____

    What would you do to avoid detection in the future? _____

    What is the biggest risk you ever took in trying to smuggle drugs into the country? _____

    Why did you take that risk? _____

    Do you think about getting caught? _____

    What is the worst thing that could happen if you were apprehended by law enforcement? _____

23. What are the consequences for losing a load? _____

    What proportion of the load is considered an acceptable loss? _____

    Is the answer different if the load is seized, stolen, or lost? _____

    What type of person do you answer to? _____

    What type of threats would they make? _____

    How do they determine that you didn't just sell it out from under them? _____

    What do you have to do to pay them back? _____

    Why do you think you been trusted with drugs? _____

    Does the size of the load you are entrusted with increase with the number of successful runs or experience? _____

24. Do you have any knowledge about other seizures that have occurred? Do you think certain organizations are targeted? _____

25. How do you learn about US efforts to interdict drugs? _____

    What forms of technology did you use to learn about or monitor the activities of the US government? _____

    How quickly do you change your tactics for smuggling after learning about new interdiction strategies? _____

26. If you were put in charge of trying to stop the illegal smuggling of drugs into the US what steps would you take? _____

   What would it take to make you stop smuggling drugs into the US?

   _____

27. What drugs have you ever used in your lifetime?
   Cocaine   Heroin   Marijuana
   Other (specify) _____   None _____

   How regularly do you use drugs?   Daily   Weekly   Monthly

   G. How are you supporting your family while in prison?

   _____

   What will happen to you after you finish your sentence? _____

   If deported?

   Will you go back to smuggling drugs? _____

28. Is there any other thing I should know about interdicting drug smuggling that we have not mentioned during this conversation?

   _____

   _____

[120 MINUTES]

Date of Interview: _____

Location: _____

Interviewer: _____

Appendix 2
Study Design

The instrument was designed to accomplish two goals. The first was to collect background information on the way smuggling operations are organized and on the specific roles in each type of operation (e.g., transporting the drugs by commercial vessel, private vessel, plane), as well as on individual experiences in the smuggling world (number of times a person was involved in smuggling drugs, his roles in the various offenses, his decision-making authority), to help interpret what is learned about balancing the risks associated with smuggling drugs. The second goal was to try to understand smugglers' perceptions of risk and the level of risk that would deter them from continuing an operation.

To achieve these goals, an instrument was designed to collect background information on the individual's experience of smuggling drugs and descriptions of the individual's first, typical, and last offense, focusing on his role in the offense and his role in relation to others in the operation. From this information, we were able to contextualize individual responses, and also to describe drug smuggling operations in the 1990s and the way they were organized to limit information flow and decision making and, therefore, reduce risk for the most powerful members of the group. The instrument was also designed to explore individual perceptions of the risks associated with smuggling, allowing us to compare these assessments with individual experiences and roles in smuggling operations. The instrument enabled us to quantify the level of risk that would have to be present to cause smugglers to modify their behavior. Building from Rockwell International's

(1989) methods of measuring deterrence, closed-ended questions using odds were used to identify the level at which the risks were not worth the rewards. The final instrument appears in Appendix 1.

Sample Selection

Access to data maintained by the U.S. Sentencing Commission (USSC) was critical to the sample selection process. The cooperation of the USSC allowed us to identify all persons sentenced between 1992 and 1998 and serving time for a violation of section 18 U.S.C. 2D1.1. This law refers to the unlawful manufacturing, importing, exporting, and trafficking of illegal drugs, including possession with the intent to commit these offenses and attempt or conspiracy. The USSC was asked to identify all cases in which the offender was convicted for one of the five primary charges. The time frame was limited to offenders sentenced since 1992 because our interest was primarily in smuggling activity in the 1990s and because 1992 was the first year the U.S. Sentencing Commission began distinguishing between crack and powder cocaine. Fiscal year 1998 was the cutoff because this was the latest information available from the USSC.

The USSC provided a file that included demographic information and sentencing information for all offenders sentenced from 1992 through 1998 for drug trafficking as either the primary or one of the five most serious charges. Table A2.1 identifies some of the variables provided by the Sentencing Commission for the sample.

Four hundred fifteen (415) cases sentenced for trafficking between 1992 and 1998 met our criteria. Table A2.2 provides characteristics of the sample. The majority of the sample included white (71 percent) males (92 percent) who described their ethnicity as Hispanic (55 percent). Of the non-U.S. citizens (55 percent), citizenship was spread across twenty-eight countries, with the highest concentration in Columbia (17 percent), Cuba (9 percent), Jamaica (6 percent), and Mexico (4 percent). The sample is dispersed across the seven sentencing years, with slightly higher proportions sentenced in 1992 and 1993. Half the sample was sentenced in districts in Florida and another 13 percent in New York, and almost all were convicted for trafficking cocaine (90 percent). The sample varied on a number of different sentencing characteristics. For example, 61 percent of the sample received an offense level of 38 or greater (38 is the base offense level for trafficking 150 kilograms or more of cocaine), and 60 percent received no departure status, which means that they did not provide assistance during the investigation. Only 31 percent provided substantial assistance to the government, although 61 percent received reductions from their base offense levels for accepting responsibility.

TABLE A2.1   VARIABLES PROVIDED BY THE USSC FOR THE
SAMPLE

Demographic Information: Gender, race, ethnicity, citizenship status, country of citizenship, and date of birth.

Sentencing Information: Disposition, date of sentencing, age at sentencing, district sentenced in, and total number of months of sentence.

Offense Information: Primary offense type and primary drug involved.

Criminal History Points: Points are assigned based on offender's prior history with the U.S. criminal justice system, particularly prior criminal sentences and the length and proximity to the instant offense. The number of points determines one's criminal history category, which is directly relevant to the length of the sentence imposed for the instant offense. Points are established by the probation officer and confirmed by the court at sentencing.

Acceptance of Responsibility: A two-level reduction from the base offense level may be made if the defendant clearly demonstrates acceptance of responsibility for the offense. An additional one-level reduction may be imposed if the defendant assisted the government by providing timely information or timely notification of his intention to enter a plea.

Role in the Offense: Based on the evidence of the case, the probation officer makes a determination of the role in the offense, which may add two to three points to the base offense level.

Departure Status: Identifies departure from the guidelines if the defendant provided substantial assistance in the investigation or prosecution of another offender, or because of aggravating or mitigating circumstances of a kind not already taken into consideration (death, use of a weapon, or for extreme conduct on behalf of the defendant).

Offense Level: Offense levels are calculated, using prescribed guidelines, by the probation officer prior to sentencing and confirmed by the judge at sentencing. Offense levels reflect the amount and type of drugs associated with the offense, the role in the offense, and reductions or increases made, based on the defendant's acceptance of responsibility, assistance during the investigation, and other aggravating or mitigating circumstances.

The presentence information was reviewed to identify high-level drug smugglers. Based on the literature, our interviews with undercover agents, and interviews with U.S. customs officials, variables we thought would distinguish between high-level and low-level smugglers included aggravated role in the offense (the number of levels added due to the defendant's aggravating role in the offense), criminal history points, offense level, acceptance of responsibility, and the defendant's departure status from the sentencing guidelines.

TABLE A2.2   DESCRIPTIVE CHARACTERISTICS OF HIGH LEVEL DRUG SMUGGLERS IN FEDERAL PRISON

	N =415	Percentage
Gender		
Male	383	92
Female	32	8
Race		
White	296	71
Black	95	23
American Indian/Alaskan Native	1	0.00
Asian Pacific	3	1
Other and Missing	20	5
Hispanic Origin		
Non-Hispanic	186	45
Hispanic	229	55
Citizenship		
U.S. Citizen	194	47
Legal Alien/Resident	115	28
Illegal Alien	52	13
Unknown Status/Missing	54	14
Accept Responsibility		
Three-Level Reduction	158	38
Two-Level Reduction	97	23
No Reduction	160	39
Offense Level		
<32	49	12
32–34	47	11
35–37	66	16
38–40	127	31
41–43	104	25
44–46	17	4
47–49	4	1
>50	1	0
Role Offense		
Manager, Organizer, Supervisor, or Leader	155	37
Manager or Supervisor >5 Participants	123	30
Leader or Organizer >5 Participants	137	33

TABLE A2.2 (Continued)

	N = 415	Percentage
Departure Status		
None	250	60
Upward	1	0
Downward	19	5
Substantial Assistance	129	31
Missing	16	4
Criminal History Points		
0	253	61
1 through 3	86	21
4 through 6	54	13
7 through 10	16	4
>10	6	1

To determine how the above variables might be used to narrow the sample, data for a subset of the sample were compared to the more detailed information available in presentence reports (PSRs) for the same cases. The Monitoring Division of the USSC was able to make presentence reports immediately available for the majority (93 percent) of the cases sentenced in 1998. PSRs are generated by probation officers for the judge's consideration at sentencing. A typical PSR includes demographic information, information on the instant and related offenses (obtained from codefendants, undercover agents, or confidential informants), criminal history, family medical and employment history, and a computation of the adjusted offense level. The files also include copies of the indictment, plea agreement, objections by the prosecution or the government, and the sentencing report.

Although the level of detail varied across reports, a specific set of elements was coded from each report. Since we were most interested in high-level drug smugglers, the information was used to determine the offender's level of involvement in drug smuggling and whether the offender would be able to provide information of interest. After reviewing specific cases, the reviewers found that the most useful information was the role in the offense: mules, couriers, offloaders, and those who managed, led, or supervised activities that were unrelated to the transport were viewed as not as favorable as those with more active roles in the actual transport of the drugs to the United States. The role of the defendant in the instant offense was typically well outlined in the PSR, as it is used to make sentencing decisions. The reviewers also found information in the PSR on the scope of the operation that the defendant was overseeing and the relationship to the actual transport of drugs to be helpful in determining which smugglers would be useful to interview.

Identifying Cases for Review

After reviewing a sample of the PSRs, comparing the information against the variables in the data set provided by the USSC for the same cases and reviewing interview decisions made as a result, it was determined that the detailed information contained in the PSRs was so valuable that only a few exclusions should be made before reviewing them. The few criteria that consistently excluded cases because individuals were determined to have had minor roles in the smuggling operation included gender, U.S. citizenship status, and offense level. From the sample of 415 cases, 32 women and 53 male U.S. citizens with no prior convictions who were not leaders or organizers of more than 5 people were excluded.[1] Thirty-three additional cases with offense levels below 32 were excluded from the sample. A base offense level of 32 indicates that the person smuggled or conspired to smuggle at least five kilograms but less than fifteen kilograms of cocaine into the United States. Those who smuggled or conspired to smuggle less than five kilograms but had aggravated roles in the offense or aggravated circumstances related to the case were included. Of most importance is that this criterion included the majority of cases in which the offenders held leadership positions in a conspiracy to smuggle more than fifteen kilograms into the United States.

The result was a sample of 297 cases. The sample was not a random selection of federal prisoners convicted of drug trafficking and was purposively biased toward high-level or more serious drug smugglers. When comparing the 297 against the original 415 cases, the 297 differed in areas affected by the selection criteria. These were male offenders who were less likely to be U.S. citizens and who were more serious on variables associated with the instant offense (e.g., role, offense level). However, the group was similar to the original sample on such variables as year sentenced, disposition, departure status, acceptance of responsibility, and race.

Selecting the Final Sample

The Sentencing Commission was asked to provide the PSRs for all 297 cases and provided all but 11 cases for our review.[2] The same review sheets used to review the 1998 PSRs were used to code relevant information, and the same two people reviewed all the PSRs. Both participated in the observations of the

TABLE A2.3   A COMPARISON OF THE TOTAL SAMPLE TO THE 174
HIGH LEVEL SMUGGLERS

Variables	N =415	Percentage	Percentage	N =174
Gender				
Male	383	92	100	174
Female	32	8	0	0
Race				
White	296	71	83	144
Black	95	23	12	21
American Indian/Alaskan Native	1	0.00	0	0
Asian Pacific	3	1	1	1
Other and Missing	20	5	5	8
Hispanic Origin				
Non-Hispanic	186	45	30	52
Hispanic	229	55	70	122
Citizenship				
U.S. Citizen	194	47	44	76
Legal Alien/Resident	115	28	28	48
Illegal Alien	52	13	13	21
Unknown Status/Missing	54	14	15	29
Accept Responsibility				
Three-Level Reduction	158	38	35	60
Two-Level Reduction	97	23	28	48
No Reduction	160	39	38	66
Offense Level				
<32	49	12	0	0
32–34	47	11	4	7
35–37	66	16	14	24
38–40	127	31	38	66
41–43	104	25	35	61
44–46	17	4	7	12
47–49	4	1	2	3
>50	1	0	1	1
Role Offense				
Manager, Organizer, Supervisor, or Leader	155	37	20	34
Manager or Supervisor >5 Participants	123	30	24	42
Leader or Organizer >5 Participants	137	33	56	98

(Continued)

TABLE A2.3 (Continued)

Variables	N=415	Percentage	Percentage	N=174
Departure Status				
None	250	60	66	114
Upward	1	0	0	0
Downward	19	5	4	7
Substantial Assistance	129	31	28	48
Missing	16	4	3	5
Criminal History Points				
0	253	61	56	98
1 through 3	86	21	26	46
4 through 6	54	13	12	21
7 through 10	16	4	2	4
>10	6	1	3	5

USCS Miami operation, sat in the same room and discussed the coding of information, and made interview decisions together. The reviewers maintained inter-rater reliability by comparing notes and decisions during the review process and ensuring agreement. The same selection criteria were applied to identify the highest-level smugglers in the sample and, therefore, the most appropriate for interviewing. Of the 286 PSRs that were reviewed, 174 offenders were identified as potential interview candidates.

Table A2.3 demonstrates that the 174 were not significantly different from the original sample, except with respect to race and ethnicity, acceptance of responsibility, criminal history points, and departure status. Consistent with the goals of the selection process, the 174 represent a more serious group of smugglers in terms of offense level calculations, role in the offense, and consequently length of prison term.

Locating the Sample

At the beginning of the project, staff members in the Office of Research and Evaluation at the Bureau of Prisons (BOP) were contacted to discuss the project, ask for their cooperation in identifying locations of a group of inmates sentenced for drug trafficking, and asked for access to approximately twenty institutions to interview the inmates. Part of this request involved a formal presentation of the project for approval by the BOP and submission of a project summary and copies of the questionnaire and informed consent form. The project was approved by the BOP via a formal letter of approval.

The BOP was asked to match prison information for the 174 individuals deemed acceptable for interviewing.[3] The BOP was able to locate[4] 78 percent of the sample as being in federal prisons and 6 percent in locations described by the BOP as temporary.[5] Another 9 percent had either been released or had passed away. Finally, 6 percent could not be located by the BOP.[6] The resulting sample included 135 prisoners. To confirm any issues with the matching process, the BOP was asked to match the 240 individuals who were not selected for interviewing, and we found that the attrition or inability to locate an inmate was not appreciably different for the two groups.

Final Selection

The BOP was asked to identify prisons for the inmates it was able to locate. Once the prisons were identified, the location and number of inmates were reviewed to identify the most cost-effective visits. Generally, locations with at least 5 inmates were selected for visits. Although we preferred to approach more than 5 inmates on a given trip, the selected individuals were dispersed across so many institutions that 5 became the most reasonable number, given time and funding. Table A2.4 identifies the fifty-one institutions in which the 135 inmates were located and the number of individuals located at each at the time of the initial match.[7] Institutions or clusters of institutions within reasonable driving distance with 5 or more selected inmates were considered for interviewing (institutions that fit the criteria are in bold or italics in the table; they housed 81 of the 135 selected inmates). Interviews took place in Miami FCI, Miami FDC, Yazoo FCI, Coleman Low, Coleman Medium, Atlanta USP, Jesup FCI, Talladega, Allenwood USP, and Allenwood Medium.

Access to Prisons and Prisoners

Once the institutions were selected, the BOP confirmed the location of the inmates at each institution and began contacting the warden's executive assistant at each, forwarding a project summary, the informed consent form, and a letter of project approval from the BOP asking for participation in the project. During the call, the assistants were told that a member of the research team would contact them the next week to discuss when the interviews might be conducted and the specifics of the interview process. The assistants were told not to contact the inmates until they spoke to the member of the research team. The research team was contacted by the BOP upon receiving the warden's agreement to the project, which came via the executive assistant. Every institution contacted agreed to participate. The

TABLE A2.4   PRISON RESIDENCE OF FINAL SAMPLE

Federal Institution	Number of Individuals	Federal Institution	Number of Individuals	Federal Institution	Number of Individuals
Allenwood—Camp	1	Fairton	1	Oakdale	1
Allenwood—Medium	*1*	Florence	3	Oklahoma City	1
Allenwood—USP	4	Forrest City	3	Otisville	1
Ashland	2	Fort Dix	1	*Pekin*	*2*
Atlanta	**6**	Guaynabo	2	**Pensacola**	**2**
Bastrop	3	**Jessup**	**5**	Phoenix	1
Beaumont—Medium	2	Leavenworth	1	Ray Brook	4
Beaumont—USP	2	Lewisburg	2	Rochester	1
Butner	2	Lexington	2	San Antonio CMM Office	1
Coleman—Low	**5**	**Marianna**	**2**	Seymour	1
Coleman—Medium	**15**	*Marion*	*2*	Springfield	1
Cumberland	2	McKeon	1	*Talladega*	*4*
Devens	1	**Miami Jail Unit**	**5**	**Tallahassee**	**2**
Edgefield	1	**Miami**	**15**	*Terre Haute*	*2*
El Reno	1	Miami CMM Office	2	Texarkana	1
Elkton	*3*	Minneapolis/St. Paul CMM Office	1	Three Rivers	1
Estill	3	Nellis	1	**Yazoo**	**6**

Boldface type indicates institutions selected for the first round of trips, and italic type indicates institutions selected for the second round of trips.

only types of institutions the BOP was unwilling to contact were community correctional facilities and camps because BOP staff members felt that the logistics would cause an unreasonable disturbance at the facility.

After receiving agreement from the facility, the research team contacted the executive assistant to discuss the project and the process to approach and interview the particular inmates, stressing the confidentiality and safety requirements imposed by the researchers' institutional review board. The specific method used to approach inmates was based on an agreement between the researchers and the executive assistant, paying attention to a process that would cause the least amount of suspicion among the inmates. In five institutions,[8] the research team was able to approach prisoners, while facility staff members approached inmates in the other five institutions. Across institutions, there was not much variation in when and where inmates were interviewed. In every case except the Miami Federal Correctional Institute, interviews were conducted in attorney-client interviewing rooms or in visiting areas. These rooms afforded an enclosed area with tables and chairs where private interviews could be conducted. In all cases, interviews were conducted between 8 A.M. and 3 P.M. because this was when visiting areas were open and executive assistants were on duty. The specific day of the interviews varied; interviews were held on visiting or nonvisiting days. Again, the decision was made by the institution and was based on space, the week we were interested in visiting, and the number of days we were going to be at the institution.

Prisoner Interviews

On arrival at each institution, researchers completed an official visitation form,[9] had their bags and personal items checked for contraband, and were asked to walk through metal detectors. Researchers were met and escorted to the interviewing area by either the executive assistant or an officer assigned to assist them. The institution was asked to bring prisoners out in two-hour intervals so that each could be approached and interviewed individually. Each prisoner was read an informed consent statement and was given the opportunity to accept or decline participation. Respondents were assured that participation was completely voluntary and that there was no risk associated with accepting or declining to be interviewed. Although the informed consent form required prisoners to sign their names, inmates were told that the forms would not be associated with the interview responses and would be housed in a separate location. Prisoners were also asked to indicate on the informed consent form whether they agreed to be tape-recorded.[10]

In all cases, the interviewing location was conducive to interviewing, interviewers were afforded the environment they requested, and there did not appear to be any coercion of inmates by the institution. The prison staff did not express any concern about the project or the safety of the inmates before, during, or after the interviews had been completed. In most cases, one or two security guards moved inmates in and out of the interviewing area and provided general supervision. In all but one case, inmates were moved and interviewed without handcuffs. The environment was very calm and controlled, and facility staff did not express concern about safety or retribution before or after interviews. In all but one facility, the Miami Jail Unit, inmates are located at the facility for long periods of time, and they seemed eager for diversion.

The inmates were not upset by the interruption and were able to make the decision about whether to participate in a short period of time. After reading the informed consent form, some inmates asked questions about the specific type of information of interest, how responses were going to be analyzed, and how the information would be protected. In a few cases, researchers were asked by the inmates to produce identification to prove that they did not work for the federal government. One inmate expressed concern that other inmates would think he was a snitch and requested a copy of the informed consent form. We spoke with our contacts at the institution to let them know that concern was expressed and requested that the situation be monitored. Other inmates requested copies of the informed consent form at the end of the interviews, saying that their lawyers wanted copies of anything they signed.

Subjects who agreed to participate seemed interested in sharing their experiences with the interviewers. A few mentioned they were already cooperating with the government in some capacity and felt they had nothing to hide. The subjects did not request additional assurances of confidentiality during the interviews and did not ask any questions or express any concerns after the interviews. Only one inmate refused to answer all the questions, preferring to tell his own story.

As Table A2.5 demonstrates, not all eighty-one inmates were approached. Only seventy-three selected offenders were approached because four had been transferred, two were released, one was quarantined, one refused to be approached by the researchers, and one prison with two inmates was excluded because none of the prisoners in the rest of the cluster agreed. On the other hand, two selected inmates who had previously been located in other prisons were transferred to one of the prisons visited. In general, the participation rate was as expected and varied by institution and whether the research team or facility staff approached the inmate.

The thirty-eight who refused to participate gave the following reasons: did not want to participate (32 percent); lawyer advised them not to participate (16 percent); did not want to help the government (16 percent); claimed to be innocent so had nothing to share (11 percent); did not want to relive the past (5 percent); was not personally beneficial (5 percent); appealing the case (5 percent); refused to come out of cell (5 percent); did not trust us (3 percent); and language barrier (3 percent). The reasons for refusal did not vary across prisons, except that the option of simply not wanting to participate was more likely for groups approached by facility staff, since the facility did not always provide the reason for refusal. The overall agreement rate across institutions was 48 percent; the researchers achieved a 56 percent agreement rate, as compared to a 41 percent agreement rate achieved by facility staff. This difference confirmed the researchers' initial impression that a higher agreement rate would be achieved when the research team was able to approach the inmate cold. Unfortunately, the low concentration of selected inmates at each institution and warden preferences did not allow us to maximize this option.

TABLE A2.5   PRISONS OF INTERVIEWEES

Institution	Number Approached	Number of Refusals	Number Agreed
Miami FCI	14	5	9
Miami FDC	4	2	2
Yazoo FCI	6	2	4
Coleman Low	5	3	2
Coleman Medium	15	6	9
Atlanta USP	5	3	2
Jessup★	5	4	1
Pensacola	2	2	0
Pekin	2	2	0
Marion	1	1	0
Terre Haute	1	1	0
Talladega★	4	3	1
Elkton†	4	3	1
Allenwood USP	4	1	3
Allenwood Medium	1	0	1
Totals	73 (95%)	38 (52%)	35 (48%)

Boldface type indicates institutions in which inmates were approached by Abt researchers. Italics indicate institutions in which inmates were approached but not visited because not enough inmates had agreed.
★The executive assistant had indicated that three inmates were likely to participate (said yes or maybe).
†Study resources did not allow for a trip to conduct a single interview.

Interview Sample

As Table A2.6 demonstrates, the interviewed population (thirty-four) is all male and majority white (91 percent) Hispanic (85 percent), and approximately half of the interviewees are U.S. citizens (47 percent). Thirty-five percent received no reduction to their sentence for accepting responsibility, and 88 percent received no departure status from the base offense and therefore did not provide substantial assistance. In other words, those who did not agree with the government's portrayal of their offense and/or did not assist the government were just as likely to participate in the interviews as those who did. The population was also a high-level smuggling group, 85 percent of whom had an offense level of 38 or higher and 56 percent of whom were classified as the leader or organizer of more than five people in the offense.

Comparisons between the 135 cases we were interested in interviewing and the 34 interviewees found no major differences between the selected and interviewed population. The only difference is that the interviewed group is slightly more white and Hispanic, which may be a function of the clustering of the sample in the South Florida area. Other slight differences were evident in

TABLE A2.6   DESCRIPTIVE CHARACTERISTICS OF
INTERVIEWED SMUGGLERS

	N = 34	Percentage
Gender		
Male	34	100
Female	0	0
Race		
White	31	91
Black	2	6
American Indian/Alaskan Native	0	0
Asian Pacific	0	0
Other and Missing	1	3
Hispanic Origin		
Non-Hispanic	5	15
Hispanic	29	85
Citizenship		
U.S. Citizen	16	47
Legal Alien/Resident	10	29
Illegal Alien	5	15
Unknown Status/Missing	3	9
Accept Responsibility		
Three-Level Reduction	14	41
Two-Level Reduction	8	24
No Reduction	12	35
Offense Level		
<32	0	0
32–37	5	15
38–40	10	29
41–43	17	50
44	2	6
Role Offense		
Manager, Organizer, Supervisor, or Leader	5	15
Manager or Supervisor >5 Participants	10	29
Leader or Organizer >5 Participants	19	56

TABLE A2.6   (Continued)

	N = 34	Percentage
Departure Status		
None	30	88
Upward	0	0
Downward	0	0
Substantial Assistance	4	12
Missing	0	0
Criminal History Points		
0	19	56
1 through 3	6	18
4 through 6	7	21
7 through 10	0	0
>10	2	6

the acceptance of responsibility and departure status, where the interviewed group was more likely to have received reductions for acceptance of responsibility, but the sample was more likely to have provided substantial assistance.

We also compared the method of transport described in the PSRs to see whether the experiences of the interviewed group and the imprisoned group could be different (Table A2.7). We found that the interview group had more experience with private vessels than did the imprisoned group, which again may be due to the clustering of inmates in South Florida, where speedboats, pleasure crafts, and yachts are typically used to bring drugs into the marinas.

A final point of comparison was of the interviewed group with the group that was approached. We found that the interviewed group was slightly more white and Hispanic, was more likely to have received reductions for accepting responsibility, and had higher criminal history points. The two groups were similar on some of the most important indicators of the offenders' participation in the offense, offense level, and role in the offense.

Data Validity

Each interview was reviewed against the individual's PSR to assess veracity by checking the consistency between specific information included in the PSR and information collected during the interview. After comparing information on the individuals' ages, citizenship status, roles in the instant offense, and details on how they were caught by U.S. law enforcement, we

TABLE A2.7   TRANSPORT METHODS OF IDENTIFIED PSRs

Methods Identified in PSR	N = 135	Percentage	Percentage	N = 34
Commercial Air	21	16	18	6
Commercial Vehicle	5	4	0	0
Commercial Vessel	29	22	24	8
Private Air	31	23	26	9
Private Vessel	52	39	62	21
Private Vehicle	8	6	0	0
Other (Mail or Unknown)	9	7	3	1

found a fair amount of consistency between the information available and that provided during the interviews.

All participants in the study accurately identified the current offenses for which they were imprisoned. Subjects probably assumed that we possessed at least this much of their file. Perhaps more surprising was their high disclosure rate concerning past offenses. Fully 94 percent of subjects' criminal history responses were consistent with those indicated on the PSRs.

Most demographic information gathered through the interviews was consistent with the PSRs. The majority of discrepancies dealt with educational background; 18 percent of the respondents provided responses to questions about their educational backgrounds that did not match the PSRs. These participants indicated a level of education that exceeded the level reported on the PSRs.

A slightly higher percentage (24 percent) described their roles in the offense as being less than that indicated in the PSRs. This result probably has more to do with the ambiguity of the PSR terms *manager* and *supervisor* than with respondents' possible misrepresentation of their roles. Because most interviews produced detailed explanations of subjects' roles in the offenses, we were able to confirm that discrepancies between reported roles and roles as indicated on the PSRs were likely a matter of semantics.

Data Analysis

On completion of the interviews, interview forms and signed informed consent forms were stored in a locked safe at the research offices. Tapes were transcribed, and texts were entered into the Atlas TI qualitative software package. The interviews conducted in Spanish were first translated into English and then coded with the rest of the interviews. The software package allowed coders to read the text and code broad sections for more detailed analysis. In light of the research goals and the breadth of information collected, the text was coded into discrete categories and then linked under broader themes. For example, text coded as either "smuggling organization," "organizational structure," "complexity of operations," and "communication" was linked under characteristics of smuggling operations. This allowed us to tag the text with descriptors and then organize the descriptors around our discussion themes. As the text was grouped within themes, commonalities emerged and differences were explored, which allowed us to tell a story. It also allowed us to identify quotes that were important to particular discussions as illustrations of the points being made.

Notes

Chapter One

1. The information presented reflects the views of the authors and does not necessarily reflect the official policy or position of the federal government.

2. The sampling strategy was focused on institutions rather than on individuals. Four of the five federal correctional facilities selected were classified as level I, the lowest level of security, and the fifth was a level 2 facility.

3. The authors noted that because the sample was limited to low-security institutions, potential bias may have been introduced.

4. This compares to 40 percent of all federal prisoners in security levels 3 and 4. However, this is an advance over the sample obtained by Reuter and Haaga (1989), whose access was restricted to security levels 1 and 2.

5. Interviewers believed that this inhibited the number of inmates who participated in the study.

6. The basis on which this was established is difficult to determine from the study.

Chapter Two

1. The following topics were discussed with each agent: movement of drugs into and within the United States, the organizational structure of trafficking groups, methods of conveyance, intelligence activities, motivation, U.S. enforcement activities, and their perceptions of smuggler responses to risk.

2. This included a complete security-level tour of the Port of Miami, the Miami International Airport, Customs airborne operations, Customs operations in the Bay of Miami and the Miami River, and the Fort Lauderdale operation front. In addition, the authors met with DEA, FBI, and U.S. attorney representatives in the Southern District of Florida.

3. This change proved important during the interviews. Smugglers were surprised to learn that they could be convicted even if they never touched the drugs.

4. Women, U.S. citizens with no prior convictions who were not leaders or organizers of more than five people, and cases with offense levels below 32 were consistently identified by reviewers as having supporting roles in the offense and as lacking direct decision making and were, therefore, excluded.

5. The USSC could not access eleven PSRs.

6. The Bureau of Prisons was not able to locate all individuals in the sample for the following reasons: missing information, death, foreign treaty transfer, good conduct release, in-transit, INS detainee removals, prolonged in-transit, federal writs, substance abuse treatment release, involvement in the witness protection program.

7. Selected inmates could not be approached because they had been transferred (four), released (two), and quarantined (one), and refused to be approached by researchers (one), and two prisons were excluded because inmates in the rest of the cluster had refused. However, two selected inmates were added because of transfer to one of the prisons that was visited.

8. This result probably has more to do with the ambiguity of the PSR terms *manager* and *supervisor* than with the respondents' misrepresentation of their roles.

Chapter Three

1. All quotations from interviews are indented, and the subject number identifying the smuggler appears in parentheses following the quotation. Following Wright and Decker (1994), quotations are presented in their transcribed form with changes noted in brackets to clarify meaning.

2. Two smugglers accused U.S. law enforcement of stealing part of the load because the full amount of seized drugs was not reported.

3. Math was not the strongest skill of many of our subjects.

Chapter Four

1. One latent consequence of post–9-11 security at U.S. airports is an increase in the number of security personnel, further acting as a deterrent to smuggling through airports.

2. We did not hear much about the use of swallowers as an alternate way to smuggle drugs because the sample generally consisted of cocaine smugglers who did not see the merits in transporting one kilo of coke at a time. Swallowing seems to make more sense with heroin because of the greater value of a unit of heroin.

Chapter Six

1. We hesitate to use the word *career* in this context for a number of reasons. A career implies a sustained commitment to drug smuggling as a form of economic enterprise. Even the high-level smugglers we interviewed were, at most, sporadically involved in smuggling ventures.

2. Dry conspiracies require proof only that defendants were involved in conspiring to smuggle drugs into the United States; i.e., drugs need not be found on that person.

3. It is instructive to recall that most smugglers placed their actual chance of being arrested at much lower than 50 percent, well below the lowest threshold in this question. The discrepancy between the perceived chance and the actual chance of being arrested is key in the decision about whether to offend. In this case, it appears that the gap is large enough that it has little or no deterrent effect.

Chapter Seven

1. This distinction is similar to a debate that has gone on in gang research over the degree of organization of gangs, gang members, and gang crimes. Because law enforcement generally confronts the most criminally involved ends of these distributions, they tend to see them as more formal-rational organizations. But a fuller picture of gang activity shows them to be considerably disorganized and rarely capable of well-coordinated team action.

2. A number of smugglers discussed using submarines, in the belief that they would be much more likely to avoid detection than are surface methods of transport. We believe that this was the talk of myth rather than reality. Myths are common among offenders and often function to keep them motivated and rein in the excesses of their behavior. However, a submerged craft with drugs aboard was seized in the Carribean in 2007.

Appendix Two

1. The reason these criteria could not be extended to non-U.S. citizens is that criminal histories from outside the United States are not systematically recorded.

2. PSRs must be accessed by the USSC from an off-site location. The USSC could not provide a reason why the 11 PSRs could not be located.

3. The BOP determined that one person was in the sample twice and, therefore, matched 173 offenders.

4. The USSC and BOP do not share the same computer system and do not use the same identifiers to track individuals. Therefore, to locate the selected individuals, staff members at the BOP used a combination of the USSC identifiers and birth dates. We did not expect a perfect match and did not receive one.

5. This could mean, for example, that the inmate was in-transit, on a federal writ, or in an INS detainee removal. The location of these inmates was checked two months later, and they were still not in BOP locations.

6. According to BOP officials, these cases were not missing for a specific reason and were not any different from other cases.

7. The location of inmates changed over time. Therefore, once an institution was selected, the number of inmates located at the institution was verified before the visit. Additionally, the BOP was asked to conduct additional matches before departure to see if others in the final sample were moved to the selected institutions.

8. Miami FCI, Miami FDC, Yazoo FCI, Coleman Low, and Atlanta USP.

9. An NCIC check was conducted by the prison for interviewers and translators before each visit.

10. Only one inmate refused to be tape-recorded.

References

Abt Associates. 1999. *Study of Drug Smuggling Deterrence*, Vol. 1, *Technical Proposal*. Washington, DC: Abt Associates.

Arquilla, John, and David Ronfeldt. 1997. *In Athena's Camp: Preparing for Conflict in the Information Age*. Santa Monica, CA: Rand.

Astorga, Luis. 2001. "Drug Trafficking in Mexico." Available at www.india-seminar.com/2001/504/504%201uuis%astorga.htm (accessed 8/8/2007).

Best, Joel, and David Luckenbill. 1994. *Organizing Deviance*. Englewood Cliffs, NJ: Prentice-Hall.

Bunker, Robert J., and John P. Sullivan. 1998. "Cartel Evolution: Potentials and Consequences." *Transnational Organized Crime* 42, no. 2: 55–74.

Burt, Ron. 1992. *Structural Holes*. Cambridge, MA: Harvard University Press.

Caulkins, Jonathon, Gene Crawford, and Peter Reuter. 1993. *Simulation of Adaptive Response: A Model of Drug Interdiction*. Santa Monica, CA: Rand.

Clarke, Ronald V., and Rick Brown. 2003. "International Trafficking in Stolen Vehicles." In *Crime and Justice: A Review of Research*, vol. 30, ed. Michael Tonry, 197–228. Chicago: University of Chicago Press.

DEA. 1997. *Changing Dynamics of the U.S. Cocaine Trade*. Washington, DC: DEA Intelligence Division.

Decker, Scott H., Tim S. Bynum, and Deborah L. Weisel. 1998. "A Tale of Two Cities: Gang Organization." *Justice Quarterly* 15, no. 3: 395–425.

Decker, Scott H., and Barrik Van Winkle. 1996. *Life in the Gang: Family, Friends, and Violence*. New York: Cambridge University Press.

Donald, Ian, and Angela Wilson. 2000. "Ram Raiding: Criminals Working in Groups." In *The Social Psychology of Crime*, ed. David Canter and Laurence Alison, 191–246. Burlington, VT: Ashgate.

Einstadter, Werner. 1969. "The Social Organization of Robbery." *Social Problems* 17: 64–83.

Evidence Based Research Inc. 1995. *The ONDCP Transit Zone Study Cocaine Flow Model (CFM)*.

General Accounting Office. 1999. *Narcotics Threat from Colombia Continues to Grow*. Washington, DC: GAO.

Gottfredson, Michael, and Travis Hirschi. 1979. *A General Theory of Crime*. Palo Alto, CA: Stanford University Press.

Griffith, Ivelaw Lloyd. 1997. *Drugs and Security in the Caribbean: Sovereignty under Siege*. State College: Pennsylvania State University Press.

Hedberg, Bo. 1981. "How Organizations Learn and Unlearn." In *Handbook of Organizational Design*, vol. 1, ed. P. C. Nystrom and W. H. Starbuck, 3–27. New York: Oxford University Press.

Hirschi, Travis. 1969. *Causes of Delinquency*. Berkeley: University of California Press.

Ianni, Francis A. 1974. *Black Mafia: Ethnic Succession in Organized Crime*. New York: Simon and Schuster.

Institute for Defense Analysis (IDA). 1999. *Deterrence Effects of Operation Frontier Shield*.

Jacobs, Bruce. 1999. *Robbing Drug Dealers: Violence beyond the Law*. Boston: Northeastern University Press.

Jacobs, Bruce, Volkan Topali, and Richard Wright. 2003. "Carjacking, Streetlife and Offender Motivation." *British Journal of Criminology* 43: 673–88.

Johnston, Paul, William Rhodes, K. Carrigan, and E. Moe. 1999. *The Price of Illicit Drugs: 1981 through the Second Quarter of 1998*. Cambridge, MA: Abt Associates.

Katz, Charles, and Vince Webb. 2006. *Policing Gangs in America*. New York: Cambridge University Press.

Klein, Malcolm. 1995. *The American Street Gang*. New York: Oxford University Press.

Layne, Mary, William Rhodes, and Caben Chester. 2000. *The Cost of Doing Business for Cocaine Smugglers*. Washington, DC: Abt Associates.

MacCoun, Robert, and Peter Reuter. 2001. *Drug War Heresies: Learning from Other Vices, Times and Places*. New York: Cambridge University Press.

McCorkle, Richard, and Terence Meithe. 2001. *Panic: The Social Construction of the Street Gang Problem*. Englewood Cliffs, NJ: Prentice-Hall.

Naylor, R. T. 1997. "Mafias, Myths and Markets: On the Theory and Practice of Enterprise Crime." *Transnational Organized Crime* 3, no. 3: 1–45.

Observatoire Geopolitique des Drogues (OGD). 1998. *The World Geopolitics of Drugs 1997/1998.* Annual Report. Commission of the European Communities. Paris: OGD.

Perrow, Charles. 1999. *Normal Accidents: Living with High Risk Technologies.* Princeton, NJ: Princeton University Press.

Reuter, Peter, Gene Crawford, and J. Cave. 1988. *Sealing the Borders: The Effects of Increased Military Participation in Drug Interdiction.* Santa Monica, CA: Rand.

Reuter, Peter, and John Haaga. 1989. *The Organization of High-Level Drug Markets: An Exploratory Study.* Santa Monica, CA: Rand.

Rhodes, William, Mary Layne, Patrick Johnston, and Lynne Hozik. 2000. *What America's Users Spend on Illegal Drugs 1988–1998.* Washington, DC: Office of National Drug Control Policy.

Riley, Jack. 1993. *Snow Job? The Efficiency of Source Country Cocaine Policies.* Santa Monica, CA: Rand.

Rockwell International. 1989. *Component I Study Report. Measuring Deterrence—Approach and Methodology.* Arlington, VA: Author.

Rosenfeld, Richard. 2004. "Terrorism and Criminology." In *Terrorism and Counter-Terrorism: Criminological Perspectives,* ed. Mathieu Deflem, 19–32. Amsterdam: Elsevier.

Rydell, C., and S. Everingham. 1994. *Controlling Cocaine, Supply versus Demand Programs.* Santa Monica, CA: Rand.

Schiray, Michel. 2001. *Introduction: Drug Trafficking, Organised Crime, and Public Policy for Drug Control.* UNESCO. Oxford: Blackwell.

Schiray, Michel. 2003. "Integrating Case-Studies Lessons in Business Modeling Narcotics Trafficking Enterprises. Globalisation, Drugs and Criminalisation." In *Research from Brazil, Mexico, India and China in an International Perspective: Report of the MOST-UNESCO/United Nations, ODCCP Research Projects,* ed. Christian Geffray, Guilham Fabre, and Michel Schiray. Paris-Vienna.

Sevigny, Eric L., and Jonathon P. Caulkins. 2004. "Kingpins or Mules: An Analysis of Drug Offenders Incarcerated in Federal and State Prisons." *Criminology and Public Policy* 3: 401–34.

Shover, Neal. 1996. *Great Pretenders: Pursuits and Careers of Persistent Thieves.* Boulder, CO: Westview Press.

United Nations. 2005. *W005 World Drug Report,* vol. 1, *Analysis.* New York: Office on Drugs and Crime.

Weisburd, David, and Anthony Braga. 2006. *Police Innovation: Contrasting Perspectives.* New York: Cambridge University Press.

Williams, Phil. 1998. "The Nature of Drug-Trafficking Networks." *Current History* April: 154–59.

Wright, Richard, and Scott H. Decker. 1994. *Burglars on the Job: Streetlife and Residential Burglary.* Boston: Northeastern University Press.

Wright, Richard, and Scott H. Decker. 1997. *Armed Robbers in Action.* Boston: Northeastern University Press.

Zabludoff, Sidney. 1997. "Columbian Narcotics Organizations as Business Enterprises." *Transnational Organized Crime* 3: 20–49.

Zaitch, Damian. 2002. *Trafficking Cocaine: Colombian Drug Entrepreneurs in the Netherlands.* The Hague, Netherlands: Kluwer.

Index

Scott H. Decker is Professor of Criminology and Criminal Justice at Arizona State University. He is author of *Life in the Gang: Family, Friends and Violence,* which received the Outstanding Book Award by the Academy of Criminal Justice Sciences in 1998.

Margaret Townsend Chapman is an Associate at Abt Associates Inc.